GHOST INVESTIGATOR

Volume 8
Back into the Light

Written by
Linda Zimmermann

Also by Linda Zimmermann

Bad Astronomy
Forging a Nation
Civil War Memories
Ghosts of Rockland County
Haunted Hudson Valley
More Haunted Hudson Valley
Haunted Hudson Valley III
A Funny Thing Happened on the Way to Gettysburg
Rockland County: Century of History
Mind Over Matter
Home Run
Ghost Investigator, Volume 1: Hauntings of the Hudson Valley
Ghost Investigator, Volume 2: From Gettysburg, PA to Lizzie Borden, AX
Ghost Investigator, Volume 3
Dead Center
Rockland County Scrapbook
Ghost Investigator, Volume 4: Ghosts of New York and New Jersey
Ghost Investigator, Volume 5: From Beyond the Grave
Ghost Investigator, Volume 6: Dark Shadows
Ghost Investigator, Volume 7: Psychic Impressions

The author is always looking for new ghost stories. If you would like to share a haunting experience go to:

www.ghostinvestigator.com

Or write to:

Linda Zimmermann
P.O. Box 192
Blooming Grove, NY 10914

Or send email to: linda@gotozim.com

Ghost Investigator, Volume 8: Back into the Light
Copyright © 2008 Linda Zimmermann

All rights reserved. This book may not be reproduced in whole or in part without permission.

ISBN: 978-0-9799002-1-1

CONTENTS

A Patriot's Home	1
Borland House	8
The Un-vestigation	29
Boscobel	37
Fort Montgomery	44
Stewart House	68
Ulster County Jail	75
Sins of the Father	99

Introduction

Darkness comes in many forms. It can creep across the landscape at nightfall, turning a previously pleasing view into foreboding and frightening blackness. It can also come from within, when the human heart can no longer bear some awful weight and the mind then sinks into the darkness of despair.

Then there are the darker forces around us, spirits of the dead who often choose to invade our homes. Some have no ill intentions, yet their mere presence unsettles the living. There are those, whoever, who seek us out as victims of their wrath, hoping to feed off the energy of our fear.

This book contains cases involving the dead who are both simply harmlessly going about their business, as well as the more sinister entities who seek to make the lives of homeowners a living hell. There is also the amazing case of a famous Revolutionary War battlefield where soldiers relive their final hours, and the fascinating case of the jail where the suicides of desperate prisoners have left terrifying spirits who remain locked to their misery.

For those spirits who are lost and confused, I have the utmost compassion and pray for their release. For those who intentionally victimize innocent occupants, I have recently lost patience. I am increasingly finding that in such cases the homeowner must fight back—not with a vindictive manner to cast these spirits to who-knows- where, but with the force of light.

Back into the Light evokes many images, first and foremost for this book it is both a concept and a way of life. When people employ all the mental, emotional, and physical powers of light and positivity, the darkness loses its grip and has no choice but to leave or be transformed. People who find themselves in the midst of a negative haunting have an obligation to themselves and their loved ones to fight back and regain control of their homes and lives.

On a personal level, *Back into the Light* is an opportunity for me to practice what I preach. After the devastating losses of loved ones last year, this year I find myself within another form of darkness—the fear of a personal health crisis. As I write these words I face surgery, and who knows what else, but I am trying to hold myself above the darkness. It will be one of the toughest battles I have ever fought, but I have every intention of fighting on.

To those who look at ghost stories as amusing entertainment, enjoy yourselves with this book! For those who look for deeper meanings in the affairs of restless spirits, there is plenty of paranormal meat within these pages in which you can sink your teeth. As I have said in the past, there is much the dead can teach the living.

In closing, remember it is always best to stay along the path of light. It's not always easy with forces poised to tackle you at every step, but when all is said and done, at least you will have the satisfaction of having fought with the right team.

Linda Zimmermann
August 2008

A Patriot's Home

While conducting a public ghost hunt at the Shanley Hotel in Napanoch, New York, one of the participants, Denise, told me some fascinating stories about the old house in which she lived. I asked if she would be interested in an investigation, which she was, and then asked where she lived. As we were about an hour from where I lived, I hoped it wasn't too much farther away. To my surprise, the location turned out to be less than a mile from my house, on a street I passed just about every day.

It was a memorable Sunday in January when I first went to Denise's house in Chester, New York—because the NY Giants had finally won a playoff game for the first time in seven years! As football comes before ghost hunting, I had arranged to arrive at the house in the early evening (having given a sufficient buffer in case there had been overtime). The sun had just set and it was starting to get cold again, but before the car heater had a chance to warm up I was already turning onto her street. Although I had passed that street for ten years, I had never been all the way down it, and noticed that like in the rest of the county there was a lot of recent construction.

However, at the end of this long road full of new houses stands one of the oldest homes in Orange County. The original structure had been built around 1750, when residents were still saying "God save the King" and many future patriots were still in diapers. Over the years the structure evolved into two stories of living space, with the former ground floor kitchen becoming the basement.

Records indicate that the man who constructed the earliest section was Elihu Marvin, who along with his son, Seth, fought for the patriot cause during the Revolutionary War, as a general and captain, respectively. He later became an elder for the town of Chester, and an 1850 map of the county showed a number of Marvin families around the area. The property was passed through the female line, and the names changed to Dawes and Murray as the generations lived and died on the land.

When Denise's parents bought the house in the 1980s, it was the first time in over 200 years that the place left the ownership of

The original kitchen fireplace is now on the basement level. Note the old hand-hewn wooden beams.

the original family. But don't think the haunted activity began because the spirits of Elihu and his descendants were angry that there were outsiders in their home. Apparently, the Marvins, Dawes, and Murrays were not averse to haunting their own family members, as the place had been used as a rental property for many years because the paranormal activity was so unpleasant, no one in the family wanted to live there.

When Denise's parents went to look at the house, the real estate agent told them that she had to disclose that the place had ghosts. Specifically, the house was haunted by the ghosts of two men and a little girl.

"You're kidding, right?" Denise's father asked, laughing off the entire idea as being utterly absurd. That was the end of that discussion, and the deal went through.

Of course, it's easy to discount the idea of ghosts if you don't plan on living in the house. The place was purchased as an investment property, and for many years they rented it to tenants. Then in 1989 Denise's family did move in, and she recalled a rather peaceful ten years growing up in the place, with nothing particularly frightening occurring.

After she left home, her parents stayed for a few more years, but they moved out in 2004. While they didn't give the reason for their leaving as being anything ghostly, they had removed the chandelier in the dining room—which was part of original 1750s structure—as it had the most unnerving habit of swinging back and forth for no apparent reason.

The house stood vacant for six months until Denise and her husband, Jim, bought it. With a family that presently consists of two boys, two dogs, and three pigs, all the room and the property would be welcome. Unfortunately, they felt anything but welcome when they first moved in.

"I couldn't understand it," Denise explained. "I always loved this house. But suddenly, everything was different and I never felt comfortable in it at any time of the day."

Jim was to have an even more unpleasant reception. A retired New York City cop, Jim is not one to be easily rattled, but something certainly grabbed his attention—quite literally—the first night he slept in the house.

"I was in bed asleep when someone grabbed the calves of my legs and began shaking me very hard," he said. "I woke up and saw that a dark figure had a hold of me. Then the figure just vanished and the shaking stopped."

Both Jim and Denise would often have the covers yanked off of them at night, and on at least one occasion a small depression appeared on the mattress as if a child had climbed up on the bed.

Another intense encounter occurred when a friend spent the night in the bedroom at the east end of the house. She awoke to see a man standing just a few feet away by the window and closet. The man was tall, bearded, and was wearing a dark uniform with a row of large brass buttons. He stared intently and sternly at her, then simply vanished. Had this been the general or the captain?

Shortly after the appearance of this menacing apparition, a few of Denise's cousins used a Ouija board to try to get some answers about the activity. One of the questions they asked was why the ghost of the man in the uniform had frightened the woman. They didn't understand the response, but it was all too clear to Denise.

The letters came up B-R-I-T-I-S-H. Denise's friend was, in fact, from England. Apparently 200 years hasn't alleviated the hatred this patriot officer felt for anyone British!

Keeping that in mind, Jim is very careful when playing his fife, which was a popular flute-like instrument during the Revolutionary War. The first time he started playing the fife in the house, he felt a heavy, physical pressure on his shoulders as if two strong hands were pressing down. It wasn't threatening, just completely unnerving, and to this day Jim makes sure he only plays American tunes!

There was another sighting near the window where the officer had appeared, this time from the outside. Denise's aunt had visited with her children. As they were getting ready to leave, her aunt was in the driveway standing by the car, and she looked up and saw a blond girl looking out that bedroom window. Thinking it was her nine-year-old daughter, she called the girl's name and said it was time to go.

Her daughter responded, but the voice came from directly behind her. Quickly turning, she saw that her daughter was standing right next to her. Confused, she turned back toward the window, but the other girl was gone. Perhaps the real estate agent knew what she was talking about, after all?

Jim decided he needed to do some research on the families who had lived in the house. He went to a local cemetery and started taking photos of the headstones. Suddenly and inexplicably, he got sharp abdominal pains that were so severe he had to go home. Later, when he had his film developed, he discovered that none of the cemetery pictures came out. They all were so badly fogged that none of the headstones could be seen.

Jim collects cameras and has been an avid photographer for many years, and he has no explanation for the ruined film. The camera took good pictures both before and after the cemetery. The mysterious and painful experience convinced him to drop the research, just in case someone wasn't too happy that he was poking around in their past.

Every family has skeletons in their closet, and many houses have things to hide from their pasts as well. When doing some work in the kid's rooms, Denise discovered burned timbers behind the walls. The structure had obviously suffered a bad fire at some point. Had one or more of the spirits in the house met their demise in those flames? At present, there is some understandable reluctance to investigate any further!

Despite the appearance of apparitions, the most frequent occurrences have been audio, not visual. At least one entity in the house has the uncanny and unnerving ability to mimic people's voices. For example, early one morning about 5am, Denise and Jim woke up to a banging sound as if their front door had been slammed shut. Then the voice of their friend Pat called Denise's name. Puzzled as to what Pat was doing there at that hour, Denise was nonetheless very concerned as it must be something important.

"What do you think is the matter?" Jim asked.

"I have no idea," Denise replied, "but I'll go find out."

Grabbing her bathrobe, she hurried downstairs. The lights were all out, and she wondered why her friend hadn't turned them on when he came inside.

"Pat, what's going on?" she asked, but there was only silence. Searching the house, she found no one. The doors were all locked, and there wasn't a car in the driveway.

As Denise climbed the stairs back to her bedroom, she was wondering if she could have imagined the entire thing. Perhaps it was just some other sound that had awakened them, and she just imagined it was her friend's voice. There was one way to find out.

"Jim, exactly what did you hear?" she asked.

"I heard Pat calling your name," he replied, wondering why he was being interrogated.

They were both shocked by the incident, and it was to happen on other occasions, and with other voices. One night when Denise's mother was spending the night, the frightened woman burst into her daughter's room.

"Mom, have you ever heard of knocking?" Denise said, somewhat annoyed until she saw her mother's expression.

"What's the matter, are you okay?" her mother asked, visibly shaken.

"What do you mean what's the matter with me? What's wrong with you?"

"You were just screaming 'Mom'. I just heard you screaming for help," her mother insisted.

Denise assured her she hadn't said a word, although it's doubtful that it was any consolation under the circumstances! This is a remarkably creepy phenomenon, for lack of a better scientific description, having the ability to recreate the voices of friends and family members. It seems to go beyond simply trying to get the attention of the living, as the alleged frantic call for help frightened Denise's mother. This is clearly a very interactive haunting—the spirits know everyone's voices, and just what buttons to push to get a reaction.

Fortunately, the two boys have not been bothered by the ghosts. The only incident was when one of Denise's young sons came up to her and casually said, "My friend in the black shirt is sitting in the dining room."

Of course, no one was there, and it was the only time the boy mentioned his "friend." Had there been more encounters that the boy never mentioned? If so, his matter-of-fact attitude indicated that he wasn't the least bit frightened, so Denise didn't ask any questions that might alarm her son.

There have been other incidents with family members and friends who have come to the house, but for the most part these people simply get uncomfortable feelings, particularly like they are not alone. These feelings most often occur in the dining room and that upstairs bedroom where the figures have been seen. Such sensations can be frightening, but it's never threatening.

On my brief investigation, the most frightening thing that happened was when I stepped on a piece of bubble wrap in the dark. A tall figure in a uniform would have been nothing after that! I did find some high EMF readings by the fireplace in the dining room, but Jim and I tracked down some electrical wiring beneath it in the basement that was most likely the cause.

It was difficult to hear if anything unusual was going on, as the boys were at home, and one was playing a very lively video game. However, I was able to set up a camcorder in the relative quiet of the mysterious upstairs bedroom. I set my Trifield meter on Denise's altar table (she is a Wiccan), and I found it interesting that she located this in the spot where two spirits have been seen. The meter did go off a couple of times, but unfortunately, neither the general nor the little girl made an appearance.

The more investigations I do, the less and less surprised I am that old homes such as this are haunted. In fact, it seems as though any place where people have lived (and more importantly, died) for several generations is bound to have a few things go bump in the night.

In the case of this patriot's house in Chester, there's over 250 years of human drama that has left an imprint on the structure. Fortunately for Denise's family, the activity isn't sufficient to drive them from their home, and things have been mercifully quiet for a while. As long as no one hoists the Union Jack and starts signing "God Save the King," I think this is one place where the living and the dead can peacefully co-exist.

The altar table in the bedroom where the figure of the soldier and little girl have been seen standing near the closet on the right side of the window.

Borland House

Montgomery, New York, is one of those small towns that is off the beaten path and doesn't offer any major retailers or big box stores. In today's world that would be sufficient to keep a lot of people away. However, there are many magnificent homes dating back to the 1700s that still attract discerning residents, and perhaps a few discerning spirits, as well.

In 2004, Carol and Bill purchased the stately Borland House on Clinton Avenue and turned it into a lovely bed & breakfast. It isn't known who built the original house in 1789, but Charles Borland, Jr. purchased the property in the 1820s and rebuilt the majority of the structure (on the old stone foundation) into a more expansive and elaborate Greek Revival style.

The beautiful Borland House in historic Montgomery, NY.

Borland was a lawyer, a Brigadier general, and a U.S. Congressman who contributed his talents to the building of the Erie Canal. He and his wife, Isabella Hill, and other family members are buried in the local cemetery, but there's a good chance that not all the Borlands have left the building. In one of the rooms (now known as the Hanlon bedroom, after owners from the late 1800s), someone saw a woman seated by the fireplace, brushing the hair of a young girl. Was this just a snapshot from the past, or is it an active haunting by spirits who remain from a family long ago placed beneath the ground?

The Hanlon Bedroom.

Another more recent resident may also be watching over the home he loved. A woman with psychic abilities, and no prior knowledge of the place, entered the house one day and stated that, "I want to come into the dining room, but Henry won't let me." A fascinating statement, considering no one visible was standing in the dining room. Fascinating also, because the man who owned the house for much of the 20th century was named Henry.

The doorway to the dining room.

The woman also said that, "Henry is very angry about the mantel." She had absolutely no idea what that meant, but Carol and Bill certainly did. About a month earlier, the Borland House was part of a Christmas open house tour, and one man who attended had a confession to make. He said that he had a fireplace mantel that came from the house, but as soon as he got another one, he would return it to where it belonged. Sure enough, on the ground floor there is a fireplace that had been bricked over, and the mantel had been removed. Obviously, Henry was not happy about this "theft"!

Had the woman simply made a lucky guess by choosing the name Henry? Had the missing mantel (from a room she had never seen) been merely a remarkable coincidence? There was one way to find out.

Carol and her son made an interesting discovery one day; a box of old photos and documents that had belonged to Henry and his wife, Gladys. It was a wonderful collection of portraits, candid shots of family and friends, Henry's birth certificate, and his father's naturalization papers. As the psychic seemed able to describe Henry's appearance in great detail, Carol decided to set up a little test. She showed the woman some of the old photos, and without hesitation she was able to easily identify which one was Henry!

Henry may have had some cause to be overprotective of his home, as the next owners were somewhat less than respectful of the historic old structure—as was evidenced by the shocking pink paint they used to cover every surface in the Hanlon bedroom. They coated the beautiful fireplace mantel, the fine crown moulding, the window frames, everything! Carol and Bill restored the room to its former elegance, but kept the inside of the window frames in the hideous color, just as an amusing reminder.

That same family had also piled stuff so high and had so cluttered the back of the main hallway that it wasn't until after Carol and Bill moved in that they realized there was another beautiful doorway and windows identical to the front entrance, as well as a another closet! Apparently, those owners' personal lives were also quite messy, as the marriage ended in divorce and the house had to be sold. Quite often, emotional turmoil stirs up haunted activity, but these owners said nothing about any strange happenings at the closing. (Which, of course, doesn't mean they hadn't experienced anything, they just didn't disclose it.)

Fortunately, the house didn't require any major renovations, but it did require a lot of cosmetic work, and another bathroom was added. One of the plumbers who worked on the house needed to

Henry bears a striking resemblance to Leonardo DiCaprio.

spend a considerable amount of time in one of the small rooms at the back of the basement. The man, who Carol described as being "a macho, down to earth" kind of guy, would have been the last person one would suspect of believing in ghosts. Nonetheless, one day he confessed that the room gave him "the creeps" and he always experienced "bad feelings" there.

On my first investigation at the house, I mentioned to Carol and Bill that some houses have activity that appears to be focused around wells under the house. For whatever reason, some paranormal activity is linked to water sources, especially underground sources. Bill then informed me that the small basement room had an old cistern under the floor. While not quite the same as a deep well, perhaps there was some relationship between the cistern and the creepy feelings?

An infrared image of my EMF meter on the floor of the creepy room in the basement.

In 2006, an addition was put on the back of the house, and another old brick cistern had to be removed during construction. The location of the outdoor cistern is now under an indoor hallway leading to the addition, and this spot turned out to be one of particular interest.

When I arrived at the house, Carol and I sat in the parlor discussing the history of the house over a very good cup of vanilla tea, which was quite welcome on that bitter cold day. She asked about the instruments and equipment I use, so I took out my digital EMF meter, turned it on and placed it on the coffee table between us. I started to explain how the readings should be close to zero when there is no natural electrical source present, and found myself tilting my head to better see the upside down display that was facing Carol, because it didn't look like there were any zeroes. In fact, the meter was reading 2.7.

Okay, I thought, there must be some electrical source nearby. I took the meter over to the only electrical device, other than the lights, in the room. It was a CD player in the back corner of the room, but its EM field didn't extend more than a foot or so. Walking slowly back and forth, I found that the readings were concentrated around the fireplace.

Later, when we went to the Hanlon room (where the woman and child had been seen), there was a similar EM field around that fireplace, which happened to be directly above the fireplace in the parlor. Determined to get to the bottom, and top, of the strange readings, I tested the corresponding areas in the basement and the attic (and had to climb and crawl around rafters and through thick dust to do it). Identical EMF readings were found in each area, and there were no breaker boxes, electrical lines or other natural sources to account for them.

Finally, as Carol was pointing out where a window had been converted into a doorway to the new hallway of the addition (where the other cistern had been located), I stepped over the threshold and my meter went up again. I immediately asked if this was on the other side of the wall from the parlor fireplace. She wasn't sure, and asked Bill if he knew. Rather than continue to speculate, Bill went into the parlor and knocked on the wall by the fireplace. The sound of the knocking was right where I held the meter.

So, the mysterious EM field not only extends from the basement to the attic, but on the other side of the wall as well. What can account for this column of energy running from the ground to the rooftop? With no electrical lines or appliances to account for it, could it be some natural underground source that radiates up the walls and chimneys? Or is it all unnatural, or more accurately, paranormal? And is this all somehow connected to the activity in the house?

Another active place in the house is the Isabella room. One night a friend's daughter was visiting from France, and spent the night in that room. She certainly had no prior knowledge of the place, but in the morning she said that she had "heard chattering" in the corner of her room, and saw some kind of movement. In her head she heard the words "Are you a good person?" and clearly pictured a man.

After telling her story, Carol brought the girl into the main hallway where the photos of Henry and his family were hanging along the wall. The girl "almost let out a shriek" when she recognized Henry as the man in her room who had spoken to her!

The Isabella Room.

Other women who have spent the night have reported feeling a presence in both the Isabella and Hanlon rooms, but as in the case of the plumber, men are not immune to the ghosts. Bill had a healthy skepticism about the idea of spirits in his home, and one evening he and Carol were in the kitchen discussing the possibility that they were not alone. Just as Bill was explaining why he doubted the existence of ghosts, a drawer next to him suddenly slid open. It stayed open for a few seconds, then closed again!

Bill was stunned. Nothing like that had ever happened before, or since, and he could find absolutely no logical explanation for the bizarre movement of the drawer. My immediate reaction to the story was that it was a great way to literally convey the idea of opening up to the possibility that there may be more to death than many people think.

The row of kitchen drawers. One opened and closed on its own.

During my investigation, I set up my Trifield EMF meter on the mantel in the parlor, as we had already found high readings around it. This meter is very sensitive and just moving your hand near it is enough to make the needle move and have the audible alert start its characteristic squealing. Carol and I continued to discuss the house and the meter remained silent, until she mentioned something she often personally felt.

"This time of day, before the sun goes down, I just get a feeling," she began to explain, clarifying that it wasn't a bad feeling, just a presence.

I asked if the feeling was in a particular part of the house, and she said that she was rarely in the guest bedroom areas, spending most of her time in the new addition and this parlor. As she was saying how much she enjoyed sitting here and reading at this time of day, the meter gently, but distinctly squealed. Perhaps it was just an acknowledgement by one of the learned and well-read former owners that they approve of Carol's intellectual pursuits?

Toward the end of the investigation, after it was dark, I put the Trifield back on the mantel. Carol was across the room, and I was standing about eight feet from the fireplace when I said that since it was dark, we would not be able to see the needle move. I was about to add that if there was going to be any activity, it would have to be strong enough to make the audible alert sound (with weaker EM fields, the needle can have some movement without the sound), but before I could even start the sentence the meter squealed quite loudly. There's nothing like having something respond to your thoughts before you can verbalize them!

Another source of mysterious EMF was in the small basement room which made the plumber feel very uncomfortable. I placed the meter on the floor a few feet inside the doorway, and Carol and I stood back several more feet in the adjacent room. When I started asking the usual questions about anything wanting to make its presence known, the needle moved vigorously up and down. This went on for a couple of minutes, then there was nothing. The atmosphere also changed at that point, so whatever had been causing the activity had apparently made its point and moved on.

When Bill joined us back in the parlor, I asked him about earlier that evening when Carol was showing me the Hanlon room. I had distinctly heard someone moving around downstairs, as if heavy boxes were being dragged. I just assumed it had been him, but he assured me he had stayed back in the new addition the entire time so as not to make any sounds in the house.

Bill then related something very curious that had happened just a few days before I arrived. There had been an incident with the furnace (which is in front of the fireplace with the missing mantel) that had released a thick cloud of black soot. While it was a chore to clean up the mess, the soot was completely contained within the room. When Carol came home from work later that afternoon, she saw that Bill's hands were still blackened, but he soon scrubbed them clean.

Shortly afterward, she went into the parlor and happened to go over to the piano. To her surprise, there were black smudges all over the keyboard. Carol is the piano player in the family, and Bill has no idea how to play. She just couldn't imagine why her husband had suddenly decided to start trying to play the piano with dirty hands.

"Bill, were you playing the piano today?" she asked, giving him a chance to explain himself.

I can just picture Bill looking at her as if she had just asked the most ridiculous question on earth. Hadn't he just explained what happened to the furnace and how he spent all day cleaning up the mess? Didn't she know that he had no clue how to play, and certainly wasn't about to start with soot all over his hands?

Clearly it was something that had absolutely no rational explanation. Even if a cloud of soot had managed to travel up stairs and around corners, there was no sign of blackness anywhere except on the white keys of the piano, as if dirty fingers had played a dirty trick. But more on this later…

Based on what Carol and Bill had told me, and what I had found, I strongly recommended that they have psychic Lisa Ann come to the house. I had worked with her on several previous cases and knew that she would be able to solve some of the many mysteries of the old Borland house.

About a week later, Lisa Ann, police detective Mike Worden, and I were on our way to Montgomery. As usual, I had not told Lisa Ann anything about the case. In fact, I didn't even say what town we would be going to, and all she knew was that we would meet in Middletown, NY.

A few days earlier, I had been a guest on the Eerie Radio program and one of the things I discussed was the importance of not divulging anything to a psychic before taking her to a haunted site. I joked that my preference would be to pull up in an unmarked van, put a dark hood over the psychic's head, toss her in the back of the van and bring her to the undisclosed location. Resisting the impulse, however, we simply met Lisa Ann in front of the local Staples store and said nothing about the case during the fifteen minute ride from Middletown to Montgomery.

I had told Carol and Bill that when we arrived we wouldn't say anything about what went on in the house, and would simply let Lisa Ann "do her thing." After a brief introduction, Mike and I put our gear bags in the kitchen, grabbed some cameras and meters, and waited for Lisa Ann to begin. We didn't have to wait long.

Standing between the parlor and dining room, Lisa Ann immediately said that she felt that "there's a lot of people in this house" and that it was almost "like stepping into a party or event," but that some of them where impressions rather than active, conscious spirits. Without skipping a beat, her next words were startling.

"I see a lot of documents, a lot of important decisions being made here. I see things being signed…" she paused at this point for a moment. "It's almost like I want to say that I see laws being signed. I do think I want to say laws."

Shortly after she also added, "This may sound crazy, but I see a connection to Washington, D.C. to this house. I think you'll find out that there was some direct connection between someone here and Washington."

If she was looking to me for a response or confirmation she was out of luck. Inside my head I was jumping up and down with excitement. Charles Borland, Jr. was a lawyer, a U.S. Congressman (in Washington, D.C., of course), a prominent local politician, and a host of other things connected with laws and documents. Lisa Ann had clearly made an instant connection to the house's most famous occupant, but there was no way I was going to let on that she had already hit a direct bulls eye, and I stoically maintained my best poker face.

Unfortunately, I did get a bit rattled when I saw that the batteries had suddenly gone dead in my digital recorder. I had just used it earlier that day and made sure the battery indicator was good. Now, in just a couple of minutes of use they had drained. I didn't want to miss a word of what Lisa Ann was saying, but Mike had his recorder running so I ran back into the kitchen for fresh batteries. I had two sets of new batteries with me, but all of them also appeared dead. Yet later, when I tried the batteries again, everything was fine and the indicator showed the batteries were at full strength. Just one of those little frustrating things that happen at haunted sites.

Back to Lisa Ann, she was describing seeing a group of about ten men in 19th century clothing discussing important issues, some of which actually had historical significance, and that the man who "signed the laws" was at the head of the table presiding over the gathering. She also kept repeating that some of these meetings were of such a sensitive nature that lookouts had to be posted by the doors. (In the attic, there is a hole in the roof just big enough for a child or a very small person, or for a man to stick out his head and get an excellent view of the main roads.)

Later, when we were in the basement room that now contains the furnace, Lisa Ann felt that it had been used as an unusual type of waiting room—bringing in members of one faction through the ground floor side door and keeping them down there until members of the other opposing faction could be ushered out an upstairs exit. All very discrete, all very "hush-hush." As politics does involve some rather volatile and secretive wheeling and dealing, this all made perfect sense.

Another area of the basement had an entirely different feel. Upon entering one of the rooms here, Lisa Ann said that people could experience a menacing feeling, but it certainly wasn't anything evil—unless you consider the evil of drink! She felt that large quantities of illegal liquor were "stashed" here during Prohibition and that a lot of drinking took place in that room. Whoever owned the stash was very proud of the high quality of his alcohol, but some of his customers were clearly not very good at holding their liquor, and that energy of drunkenness still remained.

When we were all discussing this later on, Bill said that he had found a lot of laboratory glassware in that room, and assumed it had been from Henry, who was a chemist. Had Henry been distilling more than water down there? Then Mike (who brews beer for a hobby) pointed out that Henry's father had come from Germany, and many German families had their own beer recipes. In fact, as Mike was entering that basement room his first thought was that the temperature and conditions were ideal for making some home brew.

Whoever was responsible, and whatever was their choice of alcohol, the bottom line is that aftereffects of inebriation still linger in this place. For those who are sensitive to that energy, it can be a bit disconcerting.

Even more disturbing is the adjacent room where the plumber had felt ill at ease. Again, Lisa Ann felt that this had nothing to do with any malevolent force. In fact, it was quite the opposite. She saw a former caretaker working in that room—perhaps chopping wood—who accidentally cut himself quite severely. She repeatedly commented on how much blood had been spilled in that room. Possibly from this blood loss, or a subsequent infection, the caretaker died from the accidental wound.

The shock and fear of that accident have left their impressions on this room, and people could pick up on those emotions and misinterpret them as something threatening. Also, Lisa Ann felt that this caretaker would naturally connect to someone of a similar profession, such as the plumber, and would try to warn such people to be extra careful to avoid hurting themselves.

This was a fascinating perspective—what some might feel to be a frightening presence is actually a benevolent spirit anxious to help others avoid his fate! This once again proved that there are many complex layers to a haunting, and perception is everything. Spirits have an affinity for certain people, such as the caretaker for the plumber, and it is no coincidence that homeowners are often subconsciously drawn to places that have patterns of energy similar to their own situations. I certainly won't say that anyone is ever fortunate to encounter a haunting, but there are reasons for everything, and in some of these cases we need to ask ourselves, "Why did I experience this, and what significance could it have to me?"

In the bedrooms there were other varieties of experiences awaiting us. In the room at the front of the house there can be a sense of heaviness to the atmosphere. Lisa Ann believed that this was not the result of an active spirit, but the lingering impressions from a man who died in the room due to respiratory problems. She experienced trouble breathing, but in no way felt it was an attack—which, of course, didn't make it any less unpleasant. Again, some people may interpret this as a negative entity, but with the knowledge of what is behind the sensations comes the ability to move beyond them. In other words, if you know something can't possibly hurt you, the aura of fear dissipates.

In the Hanlon bedroom where the woman was seen brushing a girl's hair, Lisa Ann immediately smelled roses, lilacs, and jasmine, and sensed a female presence. (Again, she had no prior knowledge of what people had seen and felt in the Borland House. She didn't even know where we were going.) In the closet she believed that there had once been a secret cache of love letters, and the recipient may still project that sense that this is a personal space not to be trespassed.

Lisa Ann also felt a little dizzy and lightheaded, perhaps the result of this woman having been ill, or suffering from some sort of dementia. Whatever the cause, this was clearly a very feminine energy that during some difficult time—perhaps even the end of her life—her thoughts and emotions were drawn to those love letters. While the novelist and romantic in me would love to speculate on the possible clandestine nature of this relationship with the letter writer, the ghost investigator must simply state what Lisa Ann experienced, and how others might interpret the sensations. However, the readers are free to imagine their own Jane Austen-like scenarios.

The Isabella Room also had a female presence, but this one projected a high level of anxiety and nervous energy. Lisa Ann felt that this had been the housekeeper's room, and the woman had definitely been a high stress "type A" personality. There didn't seem to be any particular tragedy associated with the housekeeper, just years of worry and anxious pacing that left a psychic residue which women—particularly type A women—would be most likely to sense.

There was also the matter of a secret panel in the floor of this room. Under this panel was a small hiding place, no more than a couple of square feet, where Lisa Ann felt that important documents and valuable jewelry were once kept. Of course, that's what hiding places are for, but after a moment she added, "All I keep seeing now is an empty box."

Imagine our surprise an hour later when we were all talking about the investigation and the subject of the secret panel came up. We were all floored (yes, pun intended) when Bill suddenly said, "All I found in there was an empty box." Bill had not been with us, and could not have heard what Lisa Ann had said. We asked for some further clarification, he left the room for a minute and when he returned he was carrying an antique box that looked as though it was designed to safeguard important papers or jewelry. He explained that when he first lifted the secret panel he discovered this box, but it had been empty.

Don't you just love this kind of stuff? Lisa Ann never ceases to amaze me, and these investigations never cease to surprise everyone involved.

When we returned to the parlor, Lisa Ann concentrated on the fireplace. She asked if I had ever gotten any high EMF readings around the fireplace, and I told her what I had found on my first investigation, and how the readings were unusually high from the basement to the attic. She felt a lot of nervous energy around this fireplace, and saw men anxiously tossing documents into the flames

The secret panel in the floor of the Isabella room.

while constantly looking over their shoulders to see if anyone was coming. Again, this had to do with the sensitive nature of the politics conducted here, and the destruction of secret documents was critical to whatever decisions and actions were ultimately to be made.

As I write this now, I see a pattern of a pervading air of secrecy that existed inside the Borland House—the politicians and their secret meetings and documents, the hidden panel in the Isabella Room, the closet in the Hanlon Room where the secret love letters were once concealed, and the basement room where the illegal liquor was quietly dispensed. This was a place were discretion was of utmost importance, for both personal and public reasons, and that all-encompassing sense of mystery can be very appealing to those who are inquisitive and have a flair for the dramatic. Jane Austen would have had a field day in this house with all its intrigue and romance!

One of the last things Lisa Ann sensed was that some of the house's owners were great contributors to the community. She asked if Carol and Bill had any knowledge of any humanitarian efforts by former residents. As is often the case in these situations, the obvious eludes us when first asked a question like this. They both thought for a minute or two, then it dawned on them—Charles Borland, Jr. had contributed money and land to build the church that was right across the street, and he had also donated the land for the Riverside Cemetery, in which his wife was to be the first unfortunate occupant in 1845. Borland also worked tirelessly on many other public projects.

On a final note, so to speak, was the question of the dirty finger smudges on the piano keys. Lisa Ann felt that this was the result of a tipsy spirit who comes and goes from the place where he had so happily imbibed large quantities of illegal booze, and thought this was an amusing way to make his presence known. In death, as in life, the intoxicated are usually the only ones who find such acts to be humorous.

As exciting as the investigations always are, the really fun part comes when we get to tell Lisa Ann how remarkably accurate she had been. And no matter how many cases we work together, to her credit she is always genuinely surprised and appreciative of what knowledge she is able to provide.

So, considering all of the information, both documented and intuitive, what do we know about the Borland House? It was the home of a powerful yet benevolent politician, lawyer, and military man, who held intense, highly secretive meetings and negotiations in his home. His commanding personality and these highly charged affairs have left a lasting imprint on the place.

A possible affair of another sort has left a more romantic imprint in an area where treasured love letters were once kept, while an efficient yet perpetually anxious housekeeper still oversees her domain. There is the residue of fear from a terrible accident in the basement, and the heaviness of a life extinguished in a bedroom. Then there is the intoxicated joy of a wild time in history when good illegal alcohol meant good times for all.

The church across the street from the Borland House.

It is always the mystery of a haunting that I find most tantalizing, and the Borland House offers myriad tantalizing mysteries on every floor and in every room. We know meetings must have taken place here, but what were they about, and what documents were burned? Who was the woman who clung to her precious love letters, and who was the man who had written them? What had been concealed beneath the hidden panel? Who was the enterprising liquor distributor during Prohibition? Who was the poor caretaker who met his end from a momentary slip of the blade? And what on earth did the hyper housekeeper have to worry about?

I'm very glad that Carol and Bill are now the owners of this place. They have carefully and beautifully restored and decorated their home in a manner which must please all the former residents, as well as delight any future guests, and they view all of the fascinating history and personalities involved with their home with the utmost respect.

As the readers of this book obviously have a curiosity about the paranormal, I would urge them to spend a night at the Borland House. Be without fear, as there is nothing harmful here, and go there with the sense of wonder and eagerness of getting a chance to experience something unique. I know there are never any guarantees that the spirit world will be receptive to visitors, but this place is steeped in so much history and mystery that one is bound to feel something special.

If you do spend the night, or at least drive by to see the house, take some time to also stroll down the old streets of Montgomery and admire the architecture of its stately homes. If you have a few extra minutes, continue down to the Riverside Cemetery at the end of Charles Street and look for the Borland graves (about seven rows in from the iron gate at the front, middle of the row.) Think of what life was like for them in the 1800s, and what exciting things were happening in their lives and in this country.

This was definitely one of the more exciting and satisfying cases for me. In some ways it was an opportunity to step into another time. Take that time for yourselves, to experience and appreciate a place where Jane Austen would have been right at home.

The Borland graves.

The Un-vestigation

It is human nature to go into a situation with some preconceived notion of the outcome, but it is "spirit nature" to be unpredictable. Let's face the facts—ghosts don't always play fair, and they often don't play nice. This case is a prime example of a very negative haunting and an investigation that did not go according to plan.

For most people, October is a month of hot apple cider and picking pumpkins on a crisp autumn afternoon, and getting to act like a little kid by wearing some silly costume to a Halloween party. For me, October is an exercise in survival—can I actually stay on my feet and speak coherently throughout an intense lecture schedule that now spills into September and November. Not that I'm complaining, but the point is I don't look for extra things to do that month.

When it comes to investigations, I try to start scheduling them about mid-November, but I will certainly make exceptions for special cases. Just such a special case was brought to my attention in October 2006 by psychic Barbara Bleitzhofer. A friend of hers, "Betty", was having a terrible time in her house in Ulster County, New York. It sounded like something needed to be done immediately, so Mike and I arranged to meet up with Barbara and head over to Betty's place.

There had been a lot going on in the year and a half since Betty moved into her ranch house in a typical 1950s development. When she first saw the house it seemed to be just what she was looking for to start her childcare business. An educated, certified professional, for many years Betty had been employed by various schools and was looking forward to working at home.

Before committing to the deal, she wisely hired a house inspector and a roofing professional so she wouldn't later be hit by any expensive surprises. The house got a clean bill of health, she felt good about the place, so she wrote a check for the down payment. It all went down hill from there.

What the seller had neglected to mention was that the house was in foreclosure. After months of legal complications the sale finally went through. However, once she moved in, the real problems began. The roof leaked, everything seemed to break, and every penny she had saved quickly slipped away in repair bills. It was all like some awful nightmare, and one of the contractors even said, "This house is cursed!"

For a number of reasons the childcare business never materialized. When Betty tried to get a job in the local school system, she couldn't even get an interview, despite her years of experience.

During this time Betty began to sense a negative presence in the house, which became so strong she couldn't believe she hadn't noticed it the moment she first stepped foot inside. Then the noises began—footsteps and banging sounds upstairs, to the point where she was too afraid to even go up to the second floor. It seemed as though her entire life had fallen apart. It was as if something in her home was intent on ruining her life.

This was the information I received. While I always let homeowners know I am there just to investigate, not exorcise, I am nonetheless cognizant of the fact that in a significant percentage of my cases activity subsequently diminishes or ceases altogether. So, I did have some hope that we could in some way have a positive effect. Little did I realize…

We certainly didn't have cause for optimism when we first arrived. The moment we entered the house, Barbara began to shake and had difficulty breathing. Mike was uncomfortable and "on guard," and soon developed a sharp pain in his head. Betty informed us that activity had increased dramatically since she had announced to the spirits that I was coming to investigate, which didn't exactly give me a warm and fuzzy feeling. (I hear that a lot from homeowners, and I'm not quite sure whether or not to take those surges in activity as a spiritual insult or a compliment.)

We sat in the living room to go over more details of what had transpired since Betty bought the house, and we all agreed the atmosphere was very heavy, and getting more unpleasant by the minute.

"They are all gathering," Betty said. "I can feel them all gathering now that you're here."

Naturally, that's exactly what a ghost investigator wants, but the "normal" side of me couldn't help wondering what we had gotten ourselves into.

At this point, I need to explain something very important to the story. Betty is very sensitive, at least to the degree that she can distinguish between positive and negative energies. (Which makes it all the more unusual that she didn't feel anything before she bought the house.) I also need to point out that Betty describes herself as a "recovering Catholic" who currently practices Wicca.

Now before all you conservative and fundamentalist types go running for your pitchforks and gathering sticks to burn the witch, what Betty essentially does is simply honor the forces of nature, as well as her friends and family that have passed on. In many regards it is a more personal and direct spiritual path, without the pomp and circumstance that organized religion often brings to bear.

That being said, however, the practice does involve the invitation to spirits of loved ones, and once you start opening doors you never know what might enter. As Barbara pointed out, more negative entities can "slip in on the coattails" of those who were invited. This is not to say that Betty created this situation, as there is evidence that haunted activity has been occurring for many years, but if you are sensitive and engage in such spiritual practices you must be very careful, especially in a place like this.

There is definitely something about the structure of the house itself. The original small ranch house had undergone some changes and additions—such as the second story bedrooms—but nothing seemed to flow together. I tried to describe it like square food containers where you can never quite scrape everything out of the corners. It wasn't the most elegant description, but I kept getting the sense that the layout of the structure was conducive to more negative energies collecting throughout the house. Finally, Betty put it best.

"You mean the house is Un-Feng Shui-ish?"

Exactly!

Some houses are bright and open and all the rooms just feel right. Such was definitely not the case here, but we didn't have time to dwell on that aspect. We had an investigation to conduct. Or so I thought...

As we unpacked our gear, it was obvious that Mike was not doing well. He had that "knitted brow" expression. If he was on the job and I was a criminal, I would be very concerned by that look. However, after almost a decade of ghost hunting together, I know that look means there's a lot of activity at the location, and most likely something is specifically targeting him. But he assured me he was good to go, so we started the cameras and turned on the meters.

We usually begin with a quick walkthrough to identify any potential paranormal hotspots. As soon as we got upstairs, there was no question that was the place where the negativity and unpleasantness was most concentrated. The EMF meter was going off, there were icy cold spots, and the anger and anxiety in the air was palpable. I found myself making a fist and rhythmically bringing it down on top of the banister—gently, but there was the urge to really take a swing at something. (Not a typical investigative procedure.)

It was so uncomfortable that Mike didn't even want to stay up there, so we decided to tackle that area later. Or vice versa, as the case would be…

Meanwhile, Barbara was still having a hard time of it, so I went into the backyard with her for a short break. That backfired when we stepped outside and she suddenly got stabbing pains in her hand and leg. The farther we moved away from the house the better she felt, but then she started hearing voices from inside the house calling us back. We were certainly getting mixed signals!

When we returned we found Mike a bit shaken. He had decided to go back upstairs alone, but clearly felt unwelcome, to put it mildly. As he began descending the spiral stairs, some force pushed him from behind—not hard, just enough for him to lose his balance. He slid down several stairs and only avoided a nasty fall and potential injury by grabbing hold of the railing at the last second.

That was the last straw. The investigator gloves were coming off, and the spirits were going to have prepare themselves to pack up and leave. At least I hoped so…

So what did we know about this house and its history? It was built in the 1950s as low-cost housing for veteran's families. The land had supposedly just been farmland where nothing had occurred, but where have I heard that before? Who can say what happened here hundreds of years ago with the Indians, or the Dutch, or even just ten years ago?

The list of owners for the property was startling. It would have been a large number for a two hundred-year-old house, let alone for one just 50 years old. No family stayed for more than a few years, some far shorter than that. Why didn't anyone live in this particular

Mike explains to us how he was pushed down these stairs.
(Photo by Barbara Bleitzhofer.)

house very long, when neighbors on either side had been there for many decades?

One neighbor recalled that bad things seemed to happen to the people that lived in this house. People's personalities also seemed to change, especially the male residents who often grew depressed and angry. There was one man who became very ill and collapsed in the house. He was pronounced dead in the ambulance on the way to the hospital, and had only been in his fifties. In fact, this neighbor recalled, quite a few men in their fifties passed away while living in that house.

The things the lawyers don't tell you at the closing...

Then Betty entered the picture, full of optimism about her plans for the house. Not much more than a year later, this same woman had seemingly fallen into a deep, dark, hopeless place.

Then comes the day we arrived for the investigation. Everything gets even more stirred up, Mike and Barbara are attacked, and suddenly the quest for knowledge becomes open warfare. But there's one little thing spirits like this overlook—we're alive and they are not, and I like to think that the power of life gives us the home court advantage. At least I was keeping my fingers crossed that it did...

"Okay, there is no point in continuing this investigation," I said, putting down my equipment. I was definitely agitated and on the verge of raising one eyebrow, and believe me, that is one warning sign you don't want to ignore.

Mike agreed that this wasn't like any place we had ever been, and no matter how many readings and photographs we took it wouldn't alter the reality of the situation—something had to change, ASAP.

"We always try to approach an investigation in a controlled, scientific manner," I told Betty, "but there doesn't seem to be any point to this investigation. This house needs to be cleansed and things have to start changing right now!"

In many ways I was at a loss here. This was not the way I usually conducted business. On the other hand, the proactive approach felt right. I don't know why I exactly started saying the things I started saying, but I'll just tell it like it happened.

As a former chemist, it seems silly to think that burning a dried herb can have an affect on disembodied spirits. However, dozens of cases have shown that activity is sometimes altered by the practice.

"Do you have any sage?" I asked Betty, still somewhat uncomfortable trading my scientific meters for smoke.

Fortunately, she did have some and I walked with her throughout the house as she smudged (an ancient Native American purification practice) every corner with the sage smoke. While we were smudging, Mike and Barbara were sitting at the dining room table, which was right next to the spiral stairs and directly beneath the second floor bedrooms. When Betty and I got to the dining room, they told us that there had been all kinds of banging noises upstairs. Apparently, there were some spirits who didn't like what we were doing.

Well wasn't that just too damn bad…

We continued on upstairs, making sure every nook and cranny got smudged. Then we joined Mike and Barbara to talk things over. Barbara felt that there was at least one intense male presence in the house, as well as several more benign females. She felt that the females were willing to move on, but the male wasn't. As we discussed ways to send him packing there were some very loud banging and stomping sounds in the rooms above our heads. Rather than be frightened, I was actually amused. The bully upstairs was clearly worried that he wasn't going to be able to push anyone around anymore.

Among some of the more esoteric and long term options that were discussed, I had a few things to suggest that were more immediate and somewhat more down to earth. From the moment I had entered the house I felt it was like a negative energy collector and I strongly felt that physical changes were in order. I suggested that Betty get more light into the dark rooms, especially the corners, and natural light if possible. I felt that bright colors would help, such as bright yellow curtains or wall hangings. I also suggested that she have music playing throughout the day and in the evening, especially when she was alone.

This may all sound like some mumbo jumbo, but I'll never forget what someone told me many years ago: A haunting is all about the people who live there. I have found that to be quite true, as a depressed, fearful person just feeds a negative haunting. Sunlight and bright colors can definitely improve one's mood, and if you are singing along with one of your favorite songs it keeps your mind off of ghosts and prevents you from hearing sounds that could trigger fear.

I guess you could say it was all part of an attempt to reverse the Un-Feng Shui-ish nature of the house, in what had obviously become a Ghost Un-vestigation. It all made for one bizarre experience that was completely fascinating, but completely draining as well. Fortunately, Betty was kind enough to feed us, and there's nothing like a great eggplant parm to get you grounded again. (And provide you with yet another example of why it's good to be alive.)

Of course, this would have all been a ridiculous and frustrating waste of time if it hadn't all worked, and herein lies the really remarkable part of the story.

From that day, Betty began to fight back. She had more cleansings performed, played happy music, brought more light into the rooms, and was determined to take back her house. The noises stopped, and all indications pointed to the spirits having left the building.

Then out of the blue just a couple of weeks after our visit she got a call. It was someone requesting she come in for a job interview, the first interview she was able to get in over a year. Then she got two more calls and two more interviews. Betty quickly went from being willing to take any job, to being able to chose the exact position she wanted!

The house itself was transformed. The former pervading sense of dread was replaced with a feeling of a warm and inviting home. Friends even began commenting that it didn't seem like the same place anymore—which was definitely a good thing!

Betty deserves an enormous amount of credit for having the courage and determination to take her house and her life back. In whatever light you view this case, skeptic or believer, you can't argue with the results. A negative pattern was broken, and a woman was able to get a good job, change her attitude, and improve the quality of her life.

Can we say for certain that nothing will ever haunt this home again? If a haunting is indeed all about the people who live there, then this is one homeowner who has drawn a deep, spiritual line in the sand that I doubt any ghost will dare to cross.

Boscobel

If renovations can stir up paranormal activity, what effects could there be in disassembling a house and rebuilding it fifteen miles away? Such was the case with Boscobel, a lovely mansion in Garrison, New York, that Governor Nelson Rockefeller once referred to as "one of the most beautiful homes ever built in America." Unfortunately, on two occasions it was also perilously close to being one of the most beautiful homes ever destroyed in America, but thankfully the structure—and possibly some former residents—have survived to tell their stories.

The beautiful tree-lined entrance to Boscobel.

The Hudson Valley was home to many staunch patriots during the Revolutionary War, but we often overlook the other side, the many loyalists who fought for the king of England. States Morris Dyckman (1755-1806) was from one of the oldest Dutch families in

New York, but he wished to remain a loyal subject and served in the British Army's Quartermaster Department during the war.

This position may not appear to be a springboard for advancement, but he did gain valuable firsthand knowledge about officers who may have made personal profits from government supplies and funding. After the war, Dyckman was able to collect a tidy fortune from the accused officers in the form of hush money and polite blackmail. This money helped him fund his dream home, Boscobel, which was to be a showpiece of refinement and good taste, situated on a piece of property in Montrose overlooking the Hudson River at Haverstraw Bay.

In 1804, construction was begun, but Dyckman wouldn't live to see the fruits of his ill-gotten gains. He died in August of 1806, and it was up to his widow, Elizabeth Corné Dyckman, to see to the completion of her husband's cherished vision, which was to take another two years.

Elizabeth was beautiful and smart. The granddaughter of a wealthy loyalist, she was only eighteen when she married the 39-year-old States Dyckman. Not only did she oversee the completion of the house, she also managed the affairs of the surrounding farm, nursed State's ill mother and sister, and raised her son, Peter, as well as State's illegitimate son. So much for being a wealthy woman of leisure! It's no wonder that she died in 1823 at the age of just forty-seven.

Boscobel remained in the family until 1888, and was eventually acquired by Westchester County. The original plan was to create a park, but in 1941 it was decided that maintaining the house wasn't worth the cost, so the mansion was to be demolished. Outraged local citizens formed an organization that raised money to save the structure, but it was to face destruction again in 1955.

The new owners, the Veterans Administration, wanted to build a hospital on the property and the mansion was in the way. In the greatest indignity suffered by this stately home, the VA sold the "useless" building for the insulting sum of just $35. The purchaser proceeded to strip the mansion of most of the fine decorative moulding, then prepared to demolish what was still standing.

In an amazing salvage effort, people hoping to save Boscobel from ultimate destruction took apart the remaining pieces of the house and stored them in their homes, garages, and barns, and then waited for something of a miracle. That miracle did materialize, thanks to Mrs. Lila Acheson Wallace, (who had founded the *Reader's Digest* with her husband). With her considerable backing, a lovely piece of property was purchased in Garrison. The majority of the original moulding was recovered, the scattered pieces of the house were collected, and it was all painstakingly reassembled. With seemingly more lives than a cat, Boscobel was opened to the public on May 21, 1961

It truly is a remarkable story of how the house of a British loyalist came to be rescued by so many dedicated Americans. Obviously, Boscobel has a powerful attractive force for the living, but are previous generations also still drawn to its charm? According to a former caretaker, and psychic Lisa Ann, some of the Dyckmans may have also made the move to Garrison.

The palladium window.

It was a chilly November afternoon many years ago, and the caretaker had finished his work for the day. He had parked in the back of the house, and after locking up the mansion he headed for his truck. He suddenly felt compelled to look up at the house and was shocked to see a woman inside. There, standing on the left side of the large palladium window, was a beautiful woman in an early 19th century dress, slowly waving her hand at him. She appeared just like a woman in one of the portraits in the house, the portrait of Elizabeth Dyckman herself! As frightened as the caretaker was by this figure from another time, he got the sense that she was thanking him for taking care of her home.

When Lisa Ann came to Boscobel in 2008, she was walking inside on the landing in front of the palladium window when she suddenly stopped. She had no previous knowledge of what the caretaker had seen (none of us knew about this sighting until many days later), yet she stopped on the exact spot where the caretaker claimed Elizabeth was standing. She said that she saw a woman standing there looking out the window. She felt that it was the wife of the original builder and she liked to look out at her property, especially in the final days of the illness that took her life. At the time, this was very interesting information, but it was not until we heard from the caretaker that we realized just how remarkable it was.

Lisa Ann said something else astonishing at that spot. She asked if one of the original owners had died before the house was completed! Of course, that was the fate of States Dyckman, who died two years before Boscobel was finished in 1808. There would be more evidence that States was in the house, and that would be found in the dining room. Here, Lisa Ann saw a man sitting near a window. He was very "somber" because he was contemplating "some anniversary connected with the house." I think the 200th anniversary of the completion of Boscobel qualifies as a rather significant anniversary!

It is extraordinary to think that States Dyckman never lived to see this house completed, yet managed to find his home in another place and time. Is he somber because he was unable to enjoy this house in life, or because all he knew has been long gone for centuries? And why does Elizabeth remain by the window; does she want to keep a watchful eye on everything and make sure the house never again faces ruin?

In addition to the dining room and palladium window, Lisa Ann felt two other active locations. One was by the front door, where she

The palladium window is in front of the landing on the main staircase.

sensed a nervous, confused, and agitated housekeeper. The woman was very concerned, as the place was once again undergoing some

Does the housekeep still keep watch by the front door?

renovations, and this stirred up considerable anxiety for the housekeeper who was used to having everything in its proper place. The other area of the house was the second floor, where Lisa Ann kept hearing the sounds of children happily running around and playing.

There were many other impressions of the past throughout the house; brief glimpses into the lives and events of the people who once called this place home. While there were obviously the usual trials and tribulations of life, overall, everything felt very positive. As Lisa Ann put it, there was a "wonderful energy here, not like some of the other places" I take her!

Boscobel has so many fascinating stories to tell, from the British loyalist who built one of America's most beautiful homes, to the struggles of his widow to manage the family and all of their business affairs, to a ruined shell that came back to life thanks to the tireless efforts of so many people who loved this place and realized its historic and aesthetic importance.

Why shouldn't the people who loved this place the most, States and Elizabeth Dyckman, still be together in their beloved home? Perhaps they are not alone, either, and spend their time with others who once worked, or laughed and played here. The very existence of Boscobel today exemplifies the determination of the human spirit to persevere, and that holding onto what you love may be more than just a lifelong pursuit…

Does States Dyckman sit in the chair against the wall (in the center of this photo) in the dining room?

Fort Montgomery

For those of you who are familiar with my work, you know that I have a passion for history. I can recall in the third grade that one of my favorite books was about the history of the Roman Empire. I now realize that this is not the norm for most eight-year-olds, but then ghost hunting is not the norm for most adults, either, so I obviously have never bowed to convention.

I am the happiest of ghost investigators then, when I can pursue my interest in the paranormal at an historic site, and you can't get much more historic in New York's Hudson Valley than a Revolutionary War fort constructed on top of an ancient Indian camp site. Therefore, when I was contacted by the staff of Fort Montgomery State Historic Site because there were some strange occurrences on the grounds and in the new visitor center, I enthusiastically agreed to come as soon as possible.

Now I know everyone wants to jump right into all the spooky parts, but it would really be helpful if you had some background information on the site, so you can appreciate what men did here. And of course, the more you know about what happened at a location, the better prepared you are to find all the spooky parts!

Excerpt from my book *Rockland County Scrapbook*:

The Battle of Stony Point gets a lot more "publicity" than the Battle at Fort Montgomery (and Fort Clinton, just across the creek to the south). Even though the fight at Stony Point was on a much smaller scale, it did have something the other battle lacked—a patriot victory. However, even though American forces were defeated at Forts Montgomery and Clinton, it does not diminish the courage and fortitude displayed by the men who faced such overwhelming odds.

On October 6, 1777, a force of about 3,000 British troops began assaulting the two forts. The combined American defenders numbered about 600, with only half of them army regulars, the rest being local militia. Despite the uneven numbers, the fortifications and artillery helped hold back the British, but by late afternoon it was obvious that it would only be a matter of time.

To prevent "further effusion of blood," British Lieutenant Colonel Mungo Campbell approached with a flag of truce and offered the Americans terms—if they surrendered immediately, they would all receive good treatment. An American officer, Colonel William Livingston, is said to have boldly replied to Campbell that if the British surrendered immediately, they would also be treated well.

Apparently, Campbell was not amused by the American sense of humor, and the attack was renewed. Unfortunately for Campbell, he was to discover just how determined the Americans were to fight on, as he was killed leading his men against one of the redoubts of Fort Montgomery. Fighting was fierce, and acts of bravery were recorded on both sides, although perhaps none can compare with that of American Lieutenant Timothy Mix.

As the British began to overrun Fort Montgomery, he prepared to fire his cannon. At that moment, a shot blew off his right hand. Without hesitating, he grabbed a match with his left hand and fired the cannon right into a group of about forty British troops, with deadly effect. (Timothy Mix survived, and lived until 1824.)

As evening fell, the British gained entry into both forts and overwhelmed the defenders with their superior numbers in brutal hand-to-hand combat. (At Fort Montgomery, the majority of this fighting occurred in the areas of the Round Hill and North Redoubts.) Under the cover of darkness, some of the Americans were able to escape, but of the 600 at the two forts, an estimated 350 were killed, wounded or captured. And despite the promises of fair treatment, the prisoners were sent to the infamous Sugar House in New York City, and to floating prisons known as "hell ships" where many died of starvation and disease.

Of the 3,000 British troops engaged, there were about 190 casualties. The Battle of Fort Clinton and Fort Montgomery was a satisfying victory for them, and they occupied the captured forts for three weeks. However, after news came of Burgoyne's surrender they were ordered back to New York City, at which point the redcoats set fire to all the structures and reduced both forts to rubble. Ultimately, the British campaign in New York would be a failure as the Americans were able to prevent reinforcements from reaching Burgoyne, thanks in part to the brave efforts of the men who fought and died here.

The view from the Grand Battery of Fort Montgomery looking south down the Hudson River. With the narrow twists and turns in the river at this point, and the steep hills, it's apparent why this site was chosen by the American's as a defensive position. (That's the Bear Mountain Bridge spanning the river.)

While there are several firsthand accounts describing the events of the battle, there is still one very intriguing mystery—what happened to all the bodies from Fort Montgomery? It has been a popular legend in the area that the corpses of the soldiers from the battle were thrown into Hessian Lake (to the south, by the present Bear Mountain Inn). For many years the lake was called Bloody Pond as a result, with the name later changed to reflect the remains of the Hessian mercenaries that were allegedly concealed in its depths.

However, while that could be a possibility for the those killed at Fort Clinton, which is much closer, the very knowledgeable staff at Fort Montgomery pointed out that it is highly unlikely that the British would take the time and considerable effort to gather all the bodies from Fort Montgomery, carry them across the creek and down to Hessian Lake. What is more likely is that they would either leave the rebels where they fell, or toss them into the closest body of water. And according to the eyewitness account of an army chaplain named Dr. Dwight, who visited the sites of the forts a few months after the battle, that's exactly what was done. The following account is both chilling and provocative, in the sense that there are most likely many bones somewhere beneath the feet of all the tourists who walk the battlefield today.

Dr. Dwight wrote:

"I went down the river in company with several officers, to examine the forts Clinton and Montgomery, built on a point six or eight miles below West Point, for the defence of the river. The first object which met our eyes, after we left our barge and ascended the bank, was the remains of a fire kindled by the cottagers of this solitude, for the purpose of consuming the bones of some of the Americans who had fallen at this place, and had been left unburied. Some of these bones were lying partially consumed round the spot where the fire had been kindled; and some had evidently been converted into ashes.

"As we went onward, we were distressed by the fetor of decayed human bodies. To me this was a novelty; and more overwhelming and dispiriting than I am able to describe. As we were attempting to discover the source from which it proceeded, we found, at a small distance from Fort Montgomery, a pond of a moderate size, in which we saw the bodies of several men, who had been killed in the assault upon the fort. They were thrown into this pond, the preceding autumn, by the British, when probably the water was sufficiently deep to cover them. Some of them were covered at this time; but a depth so small, as to leave them distinctly visible. Others had an arm, a leg, and a part of the body above the surface. The clothes which they wore when they were killed, were still on them; and proved that they were militia; being the ordinary dress of farmers. Their faces were bloated and monstrous; and their postures were uncouth, distorted, and in the highest degree afflictive.

"My companions had been accustomed to the horrors of war, and sustained the prospect with some degree of firmness. To me, a novice in scenes of this nature, it was overwhelming. I surveyed it for a moment and hastened away. From this combination of painful objects we proceeded to Fort Clinton, built on a rising ground, at a small distance further down the river. The ruins of this fortress were a mere counterpart of those of Fort Montgomery. Every combustible in both had been burnt; and what was not, was extensively thrown down. Every thing which remained was a melancholy picture of destruction."

Several things become apparent from this account. First, the British had little regard for their enemy—particularly the local militia—and made no efforts to giving these men a proper burial. Also, the "pond of a moderate size" a "small distance from Fort Montgomery" where the corpses of the militia were dumped cannot possibly be Hessian Lake, because that lake, as was pointed out earlier, is on the other side of the Popolopen Creek to the south, nearer Fort Clinton. When Dr. Dwight looked upon these bloated corpses sticking out of the shallow water, he was very close to the remains of Fort Montgomery, and had yet to go "further down the river" to Fort Clinton.

So where, then, was this small, nearby body of water? This is where it pays to do your homework when searching for potential paranormal hotspots. A former manager of the site had thoroughly researched the history of the battle, and then carefully walked the grounds of the fort and immediate surrounding area, finding a few potential locations along the northern stretch of the grounds that could have contained ponds that would vary in depth depending upon the season. Over the years, the bodies would have decayed and the bones would have been covered by layers of leaves and silt, finally being buried and out of sight. Without excavating, however, it's all speculation.

While their actual location isn't clear, one thing is certain—the remains of these brave soldiers are still there today. Perhaps the spirits of these men who suffered the indignity of being unceremoniously tossed into a shallow pond, or left in the open to be a feast for scavenging animals, are at the root of the activity in the area today? Perhaps they are still searching for respect and acknowledgement for their courage, and a proper burial?

The angled walls of one of Fort Clinton's redoubts.

There are many possibilities, especially considering what was on the land long before the first stone of the fort was put in place. Inside the walls of the fort is one very large rock that Native Americans had once used for shelter (there are two such rocks on the grounds), as was evidenced by the many artifacts that were uncovered inside. Other signs of old Indian campgrounds have been found by the Grand Battery, and most recently while digging for the foundation of the visitor's center.

Were the spirits of these ancient residents already present long before the fort was built? It is often the case that there are many layers, both literally and figuratively, to haunted sites, and there may be some clues to support this idea of Indian spirits, but more on that later. First, we need to examine what began happening when the visitor center opened.

The new visitor's center at Fort Montgomery.

Every new building will have problems, especially when high tech equipment is now part of everyday construction. It can also take a full year to recognize the normal sounds associated with the heating and cooling systems, the whistling or knocking effects of wind and rain, and normal settling of the structure. I often hear that people don't begin to notice paranormal sounds and activity until several months after moving, but that may be more of a function of the residents taking time to become familiar with the ordinary activity in the house and finally being able to recognize what is beyond the normal realm.

Anyone who has a computer or electronic devices knows that whatever can go wrong, will go wrong, but consider this:

The first time I spoke with the staff member who contacted me, our conversation was interrupted because as we were talking about the haunted activity, the line went dead. He called right back, and we joked about it being interference from a ghost, and left it at that.

Fast forward about a month later when I called him to speak about a history book project I'm working on. The conversation was going fine until we started talking about the most recent unexplained activity at the visitor's center, and suddenly he could no longer hear me. We had to hang up and I had to call back again. They haven't had this problem with the phones before, and neither have I. It would be quite a coincidence that the only two times it's happened to us was when we were speaking together about haunted activity in Fort Montgomery.

Then there are things that can't be blamed on electronic glitches. For example, several doors are often found unlocked—doors that had been securely closed and locked. This has happened far too many times to be attributed to absentmindedness, especially now that everyone is aware of the problem and makes certain that all of the doors are properly secured.

I often find that some of the most compelling evidence comes from eyewitnesses who have no idea that they are witnessing anything unusual. For example, one night people were arriving at the visitor's center to attend a lecture. One man came in and started to compliment the staff on the authentic looking reenactor they had hired. As there were no reenactors as part of the program, they asked the man what he had seen.

He explained that as he was pulling into the parking lot, he clearly saw "a man dressed in an old hunting frock" standing close by on the grounds of the fort. He looked real and solid, just as if he had stepped out of the 1700s. Perhaps he had, because he was nowhere to be found, and no one else had seen him. (Real men in 200-year-old clothing do tend to stand out, so if he had been alive others probably would have noticed him.)

Another remarkable sighting occurred just a short distance to the north of the fort in a small office building. One day, an employee witnessed the distinct figure of a British soldier as he walked through the lobby and then disappeared into a wall. Obviously, this wasn't a reenactor, either.

An infrared photo of the museum room in the visitor's center. The figures of the soldiers are mannequins, not ghosts.

While just about everyone on staff has had some brush with the unexplained, one woman seems to be particularly sensitive and has had numerous encounters. One day she was standing outside by the front doors of the visitor's center when she felt someone tap her shoulder. Surprised by the tap, as she thought she was alone, she quickly spun around to see who had touched her, but no one was there. Another employee who was inside at the time witnessed her suddenly turning for no apparent reason as it also appeared to him that she was alone, but that obviously wasn't the case.

Another more bizarre incident occurred on that sidewalk in front of the doors. As a male employee stood there talking to a visitor, this same woman witnessed a small, dark shadowy figure behind him. It wasn't menacing, though. On the contrary, it was jumping up and down off the sidewalk like it was playing some sort of game, or perhaps making fun of him behind his back!

There have been many sounds coming from the hallway that leads to the stairs going down to the lower level. Most often, there is

The staircase to the lower level, where many strange sounds are heard.

what sounds like a broom being dragged across the floor. One day this woman went to the janitor's closet to investigate and heard another odd sound.

"Okay, you have my attention," she said out loud.

Just then she felt drawn to look to the front windows. There, peering in, was a very tall, dark figure. Remarkably, she found the courage to go outside, but the figure had vanished.

"Okay, I'm outside, what do you want to tell me?" she asked, feeling that this tall spirit was trying to get some message across.

That same dragging sound that had been heard so many times inside could now be heard outside. The dragging sound seemed to move along the sidewalk around to the south side of the building, then down towards the footbridge that goes across the creek. Had some desperate man dragging his wounded leg tried to escape the battle by heading toward the creek? Or had someone tried to pull a wounded comrade to safety? The type of activity has to do with the spirit's message, and the dragging sounds heading toward the creek are clues that hopefully can be pieced together some day.

Recently during a snowstorm, this woman was alone in the building and constantly heard footsteps going up and down the stairs. When a maintenance man arrived she was visibly relieved and risked ridicule by telling him about the sounds. Rather than laugh at her, he divulged his own frightening encounter.

Several days earlier he was alone in the building and he clearly heard what sounded like people moving furniture on the lower level. He went to the top of the stairs, saw that it was completely dark and turned on the lights and started to descend the steps. Then it dawned on him—if there were people moving furniture downstairs, they certainly wouldn't be doing it in the dark! With that unnerving realization, he switched off the lights and quickly left.

There is something unusual about that lower level—and I can now say that from experience—and several employees have felt very uncomfortable, especially near the door to another stairway that leads to an outside door. It's never threatening, but there is an overwhelming and uncomfortable feeling that you are never alone.

But then, that can be said for just about anywhere you are at the Fort Montgomery battlefield…

When Mike and I arrived at Fort Montgomery in January of 2008, the temperature was in the teens and the wind chill actually made it painful to be outside. However, if you want to understand a battle you need to walk the battlefield, so despite the bitter cold one of the historians gave us a complete tour of the site. And for any of you who picture a fort as a rectangular structure on a flat piece of land, think again. Picture instead, irregular, zigzagging stone walls running up and down the very hilly, rocky terrain. Obviously, the fort's location was chosen for its strategic value, not for its topography.

We immediately began to climb a hill to reach the western section of the fort, and the frigid, dry air burned in my lungs. Mike was just getting over a bad cold, so I can't even imagine how his respiratory tract was handling the weather, but like good paranormal soldiers, we trudged along. I had visited the sites of both forts before, but I didn't realize how far Fort Montgomery extended to the west. (Route 9W intersects the fort, and you can cross beneath the road on a safe, groomed trail to get to the western section. As cars speed along and traffic can be heavy, please be careful if you chose to walk across the road.)

The historian described how the British approached the fort, and he pointed out where most of the hand-to-hand fighting occurred. What was most surprising is that so few men were able to defend such a large fort for as long as they did. With just a few hundred men, it was impossible to man the length of the walls, so both forces ended up concentrating at the Round Hill and North Redoubt.

In the Round Hill area, our very knowledgeable guide pointed out one of the potential pond sites. Lo and behold, I found a bone sticking out of the ground, but Mike thought it was most likely from a deer. Still, it was a stark reminder of what could lay beneath our feet.

We crossed back over Route 9W to the North Redoubt, and my camera refused to take a picture. I thought perhaps the cold was too much for it, but when I walked several yards away, it worked fine. Nothing too remarkable, but certainly an area to concentrate upon another time—in warmer weather!

We checked out a few more possible pond sites, and one could see sections where water had collected during heavy rainstorms. Terrain can change a lot in 200 years, so with a few minor modifications, any one of these sites could have been where the militia men's bodies had been dumped.

Finally we made our way around to the southeast section of the fort to the Grand Battery, where an impressive line of cannons once faced out into an even more impressive view of the Hudson River and the mountains rising up from its banks. The very elements that make for this spectacular scenery also made this spot a good place for a fort, as well as for one of the massive chains placed across the river to prevent British ships from going further upstate.

When the forts fell, the British cut the chain, and it's possible that some of the massive links still lie on the bottom of the river. It's also possible that the original cannons that defended the fort were simply pushed down the hill into the river, where they still may rest today. My immediate thought when I heard this was side scanning sonar and underwater metal detectors. Imagine discovering the fort's cannons and links of the chain!

As fascinating as our tour was, after hiking up and down hills in sub-zero wind chills for an hour, we welcomed the warmth of the visitor's center. While we thawed, another member of the staff gave us an excellent description of the battle using the large three-dimensional map. It really put everything into perspective, and the bird's eye view of the forts and surrounding area was priceless. Mike and I also watched the short film about the battle, which gave us an even further appreciation of the bravery and perseverance of the American soldiers.

One particular point of interest: The film highlighted unique sleeve buttons that were enameled with the words "Liberty," as a tribute to buttons like them that had been discovered on the site. The actual buttons are in a special display case by the door of the theater, and they stand as yet another reminder of the patriots that fell in defense of the fort.

We decided to set up the cameras and meters in the most active locations; the hallway on the top floor and the large lecture room on the lower level. As I was checking out the staircase with an EMF meter, I heard Mike calling me from the lecture room. I entered the double doors and immediately knew why he had called me—the "atmosphere" was even heavier than before and the feeling of a presence (or several presences) was intense.

As he began telling me about the strange noises he had heard, more odd sounds came from some small rooms off the large lecture room. We investigated, but were unable to find the source of the sounds.

As we stood silently in the darkness, I began to get an electric tingling in my right hand and arm. This has happened a couple of times on other investigations and while I can't say what causes the sensation, it seems to me to be an indication that some strong energy is present. That sense was further strengthened when we heard tapping somewhere in the shadows around us. Then my camcorder started acting up, and refused to work for a minute, then began functioning properly, all for no discernible reason.

While Mike sat in one of the chairs that were lined up for lectures, I stood at the front of the room (where the screen is located) to better observe the entire room. Just a few days earlier, Mike had told me that he was a descendant of Betia Van Dunk, a full-blooded Minisink Indian of the Delaware tribe, and a famous medicine woman who walked to the Oklahoma territory teaching the Longhouse tradition along the way.

As I thought about the Indian campsite that was once on this exact spot, I half-seriously suggested that perhaps Mike's ancestry would help us to get some sign of a haunting, if it involved Indian spirits. Within seconds of my words, a loud banging sound echoed down the stairway to my left (in the "creepy" area). It was as if some heavy object had been thrown or had collided with the glass door to the outside, with the resulting sound clearly reverberating down the stairs to be heard by us, and recorded by the camcorder. Had I struck a nerve?

An infrared photo of the exit door where we heard the loud banging noise, and where people have complained of a very uncomfortable feeling.

Our senses were certainly on full alert at this point, and there was one more inexplicable sound a short time later. Somewhere in the room with us came an almost musical sound, like two sticks being struck together, like those used in bands or for various types of native music. Later I asked one of the staff if the heating system or anything else could cause the clear, distinct sound, but he had never heard anything like it.

We ended the evening by sitting quietly for a while in the exhibit room. There were some sounds outside, but they were probably the result of the rope and fasteners striking the flagpole. Nothing else happened, although if you aren't cognizant of your surroundings every second, the life-sized figures of Revolutionary War soldiers around the room will startle you!

All in all, I was impressed by the history of the place, and intrigued by the sounds and sensations. I knew I had to return.

That return occurred in early April when it was much warmer, but raining. Electronic equipment and rain don't mix, but fortunately a different type of instrument would be employed that day—the psychic abilities of Lisa Ann. Unlike previous cases where I don't divulge any facts about the case to her—not even the location—this time I decided to send her a battlefield map and some basic information. I wanted to know if she had any initial impressions to see if it was worth the trip. And as I felt the scene of such brutal fighting and so many deaths might bring about something of a psychic overload, I also wanted to make sure she would be interested in investigating such a place.

Lisa Ann's answer was an immediate and resounding, "Yes." Just by looking at the map she already felt drawn to several spots on the battlefield and she was genuinely excited about going. I was certainly psyched, realizing this was an amazing opportunity to learn more about the men and events surrounding an important battle that happened 231 years ago.

Expectations were high, and investigation day couldn't come soon enough. We were joined by my friend Dr. Art Donohue, who has a deep interest in the Revolutionary War. His knowledge of the battle would be helpful, as unfortunately the visitor's center was closed that day so no staff was available.

It would be difficult to relate all that happened during the several hours we walked the battlefield, but suffice it to say Lisa

Ann was once again "in the zone" and became fully immersed in the events and people surrounding that October day over two centuries earlier. Below are some of the details, with the numbers corresponding to the areas on the site map.

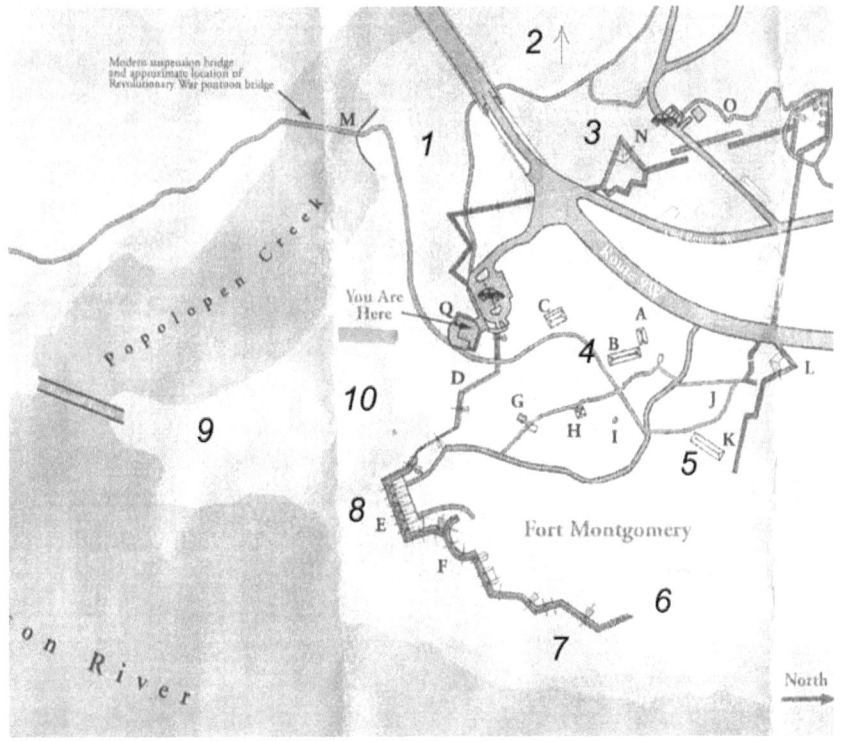

1. Lisa Ann saw American soldiers lined up receiving supplies from the creek in this area. One of the staff historians later confirmed that supplies would indeed have been brought up the creek to unload, not along the Hudson River.

2. She felt that spies for the British had climbed the banks of the creek checking out the fort at night. She believed that the Americans had expected the British forces to attack from the river, but instead came from the west over land. This was correct, and Art pointed out the trail the British troops had used.

3. Shed or barn with horses in this area.

*In addition to what Lisa Ann saw and felt, it's equally important to note what she did *not* feel. While it is believed that some of the heaviest fighting occurred at the Round Hill, West, and North Redoubts, there were no strong impressions at these locations. At first I was puzzled, but then the other side doesn't always play by the rules of our expectations. There would be important messages and clues to be revealed, but in the manner of their choosing, and for reasons that would ultimately make far more sense.

4. Lisa Ann connected strongly with a lower ranking American officer, John (Milton?), in the south end of one of the stone foundations. She saw him writing a letter "up above," not at ground level. At this point I told her that the building had been soldiers' barracks, and it was a two-story wooden structure, but the officers were supposed to have occupied a smaller adjoining building. She felt that John was there because he wanted to stay with his troops. The letter he was writing was to his family somewhere in the south, perhaps in the Carolinas or Virginia, and he was upset about the conduct of the higher ranking officers. His troops really loved him because he always looked out for them, but he was distrusted and disliked by the superior officers. John then showed Lisa Ann a gold button with an eagle, but she was unsure of the significance.

5. She felt that the wounded were brought to this building during the battle, but no one was treating them. The building had been barracks.

6. Very significant spot. Fire pit. She saw men "disposing of things," possibly dragging bodies of animals and garbage, and burning everything in large fires. After the battle, she felt that some human bodies had been

dragged here and burned. There was definitely death in this area, but she couldn't distinguish whether it was humans or animals. Excavations of the nearby barracks had revealed large piles of animal bones, so perhaps the slaughtering took place here. Also, if there had been wounded who died in the barracks, this would be the closest spot to burn those bodies.

*From this point, south along top of ridge she saw "4-legged wooden lookout towers."

7. Felt the strongest sensation yet, something like a wall of emotion she didn't want to cross, a sense of doom. She believed that John was killed here while trying to help his troops, possibly to tell them to go as there was no hope. Upset that some officers had already left, and that the men were lied to that reinforcements were coming. Also strongly felt that there was a traitor amongst the Americans.

* Accounts indicate that a man named Waterbury had been sent to bring Putnam's troops from across the river. He deliberately delayed in bringing the message, and the American reinforcements reached the west side of the Hudson only in time to see the forts overrun. Waterbury defected to the British the next day. So in fact, there was an American traitor, and the troops did believe reinforcements were coming. Also, many of the American officers did escape.

8. Lisa Ann felt that British bodies were buried directly in front of Grand Battery. She placed her hand on one of the cannon here, and correctly felt that it was not used in the battle. She believed the cannons were taken by the British.

9. Area of particular significance. She saw that the British made prisoners carry some American bodies to this point and hung them upside down from trees as a warning sign to other rebels.

10. Burial field. Many American bodies just tossed over the edge at this point, others buried with crude crosses made of sticks or lines of stones.

The foundation of the barracks where Lisa Ann connected with the American officer.

Words really can't describe how it felt to walk the battlefield that day and experience firsthand Lisa Ann's insights into the terrible events and their aftermath. So much rang true, and there was no doubt that so much was literally still beneath our feet waiting to be discovered. It was as if the barrier of time had momentarily slipped away and granted us the opportunity to glimpse the past in a very special and personal way.

Of course, a good ghost investigator always wants more, and as we hadn't yet set up our cameras and equipment on the battlefield, and we were unable to get into the visitor's center that day—where much of the paranormal activity is concentrated—I wanted to get back as soon as possible. A few weeks later, Lisa Ann, Mike, and I returned in the evening after the center had closed, but one of the members of the staff was on hand to let us in and observe the investigation.

The foundation of the barracks where Lisa Ann felt the wounded were taken during the battle.

As soon as we walked into the exhibit room, Lisa Ann said there was a "dizzying" amount of energy in the room. As she put it, "A lot of people walk through here, and I don't mean visitors." The media room felt "very confusing," although she wasn't sure why. And of all the artifacts in the room, she was most drawn to one gun, a fowling piece, that wasn't directly connected with the battle, but was representative of the type of guns the local militia would have carried.

To me, descending the stairs to the lower level is always an unpleasant experience, but I didn't say anything. Of course, I didn't have to as Lisa Ann immediately said there "was a complete shift in the mood" and that it was "very sad." Then at the entrance to the lecture room she saw a "cloud or smoke." It moved around the room and persisted for several minutes.

I asked if it was an entity, and she replied it was just some type of energy, some residual image from the day of the battle. After looking at it for a while, she settled on calling it a fog, and wondered what the weather was like the day of the battle. In fact, on the morning of October 6, 1777, there was a dense fog that aided the British in concealing the number of troops sent ashore from the ships in the river. Why would this "residual fog" still be hanging around the lower level of the visitor's center? Was it just another unusual affirmation that Lisa Ann was connected to the events of that day?

While no one else was capable of seeing the fog, the infrared camcorder did act strangely. It was aimed through the doorway into the lecture room, and as I stood by observing the image on the small screen, I noticed that the autofocus was having great difficulty. I tried moving the camera, zooming in and out, but as soon as it appeared to focus on an object such as one of the chairs in the room, the image would completely blur—almost as if some sort of mist was interfering. It definitely wasn't a problem of distance, as later that evening the autofocus had no trouble providing a sharp image out on the battlefield where objects where farther away than in the lecture room.

This mysterious paranormal fog was actually the least of the activity in the visitor's center that night. The prevailing experience was what Lisa Ann succinctly characterized as "a lot of death," suitably accompanied by the stench of death—not the most reassuring images when you're standing in the dark feeling uneasy to begin with!

I asked a few questions to get more clarification, and the scenario that emerged was the aftermath of the battle, when the British made the American prisoners drag the bodies of both patriots and redcoats to this spot. On this ground where the visitor's center now stands, an odd man in a white coat carefully removed personal items from the dead. He also did something bizarre and rather unsettling—he compulsively fixed and arranged their hair, as well. He didn't bother washing away the dirt and blood from the bodies, but it was important to him that everyone's hair was neatly fixed.

Slowly, Lisa Ann began to refine her image of this man, who appeared to be both an active and interactive spirit. He was mentally handicapped and had a deformed left leg which he dragged as he walked. His name was William, but the British had called him Fred, making up songs and rhymes such as "Bring Your Dead to Fred," a phrase that Lisa Ann heard over and over in her head. While he meant no harm to the living, people who were sensitive would most definitely be unnerved by his peculiar presence.

The staff member was not present during this part of the investigation, and it wasn't until later that I told him about Fred. His eyes widened in surprise, and I could see that the name had clearly struck a nerve.

"The woman who works here who feels the presence of a man in the visitor's center had named the spirit Fred," he said, which resulted in four of us standing around with shocked looks on our faces.

Just to be sure, he called her and she confirmed that she did in fact call the spirit Fred. What were the chances that this was just a coincidence?

Next, while there was still light, we walked the same areas of the battlefield where Lisa Ann had previously felt the most activity. Our first stop was the barracks where she instantly reconnected with John, who she once again saw writing a letter—his last letter to his family. He knew that his situation was perilous, and he wanted his loved ones to know his fate, and expose the conduct of some officers who were clearly looking out for themselves. Unfortunately, that letter was never delivered.

I was holding my digital EMF meter while Lisa Ann spoke and the readings were zero, until she mentioned the letter. Then the readings shot up and stayed high until she stopped speaking. Mike and I both went over the area again with our EMF meters, but there were no further readings. Apparently, talking about the letter had stirred up some energy.

My next question was intended for the staff member, but Lisa Ann answered it in the blink of an eye and with great certainty.

"Did any of the officers leave before the battle began?" I asked.

"Yes!" Lisa Ann replied, then realized I had wanted to know what history had recorded—on paper, at least. "Oh, sorry."

"That's quite all right," I said laughing, understanding that history leaves many types of records, for those who have the ability to read them.

While the staff member didn't know of any accounts of officers leaving their men before the battle, Lisa Ann continued to be certain some had. She particularly bristled at the name Clinton, as if picking up on the contempt that John felt for his commanding officer. There were, in fact, three Clintons involved in the battle—Sir Henry Clinton was the British commander, and the American forts were commanded by Governor George Clinton and his brother General James Clinton—but John's animosity seemed directed at one of the American Clintons.

We continued walking to the same spots as on our last visit, and Lisa Ann reinforced her previous findings at each location. Whatever she sensed before still lingered, and perhaps has done so for centuries without dimming the memory of the events and people—especially the people who sacrificed their lives here.

Unfortunately, as darkness fell Lisa Ann had to leave for another commitment. Mike and I would have to rely on our instruments and cameras for the remainder of the investigation. We set up first on the field behind the visitor's center, but except for a huge moth that appeared to be on a strafing run of my infrared camcorder, nothing unusual occurred. We next set up on the path along the river were Lisa Ann felt that John had met his demise. Again, nothing.

Then I placed my Trifield in the corner of the barracks where John's presence was strong, and I had found a high reading earlier in the evening. After a minute or two the meter began its characteristic screeching when some type of electromagnetic field is present. This continued on and off for several minutes. Perhaps the loudest reaction was when I specifically asked for a sign of John's presence, but even without prompting there were several inexplicable outbursts. Nothing appeared on video or audio, but the EMF evidence was impressive nonetheless.

What can be concluded from everything that has occurred in the last two years on the site of the Battle of Fort Montgomery? In my opinion, the strong emotions, violence, and death from that fateful day in 1777 have left an indelible imprint on the land. I think that also, due to the nature of the many eyewitness accounts and Lisa Ann's findings, that there are several active spirits still tied to the grounds, as well. The actual placement of the visitor's center was unfortunate, as the spot chosen has a high concentration of the energy of death, along with at least one unnerving entity.

At present, the documented history does support some of the findings, but it cannot yet support specific names and actions taken before, during, and after the battle. Perhaps someday an old letter will come to light, or new archeological evidence will surface that will help us better understand what happened here. For now, it is undeniable that something of the other world can be felt and glimpsed at Fort Montgomery.

Fortunately, unlike many sites that are not available to the public, this is one place where the curious can spend as much time as they want exploring acres of battlefield and the surrounding woods. And take your time in the visitor's center. Study the map to become familiar with the terrain and the buildings from the time of the battle. Look closely at the objects that had been unearthed from the men who lived, fought, and died here. Learn the history first, then see if your knowledge can help interpret any experiences you might have.

In a perfect world, the remains of all the soldiers—both American and British—would someday be uncovered and given a proper burial. If that day does ever come, we can only hope that the subsequent respect and acknowledgement would finally put to rest whatever still clings to the world of the living.

Stewart House

The small town of Athens, New York is one of those places that owes its existence to the Hudson River. A ferry began operating here in 1778 to carry passengers and carriages across the river, and service was to continue until 1947, finally made obsolete by the Rip Van Winkle Bridge that had been built a decade earlier. Shipbuilding began in the late 1700s and was to become an important business for over a century. The New York City to Albany steamship service also brought business to Athens, but it brought tragedy, as well.

On April 7, 1845, a sudden blinding snow squall hit the Athens area. This was certainly no time for racing on the river, but that's exactly what three passenger steamships were doing—the *Swallow,* the *Rochester* and the *Express,* all southbound for New York City. With such poor visibility, the *Swallow* didn't see the rocks of Dooper's Island off the coast of Athens. Reports indicate that if the ship had been only fifty feet to the left or right, it would have simply gotten stuck in the mud. As it was, it struck the rocks with such force that the *Swallow* split in two and burst into flames.

Many brave townspeople went down to the river and set out in small boats to try to rescue survivors. Unfortunately, due to the heavy snow, passengers flung into the water couldn't see the shoreline, and many drowned within just feet of the riverbank. There were no official passenger records, but it is estimated that forty lives were lost that day in the icy waters in front of Athens.

(Note: The wood from the smashed steamship was salvaged. It was used to build the *Swallow House* in Valatie, New York, which is on the historic register. One can only wonder if they have a ghost or two of their own?)

Do any of the unfortunate souls from this terrible accident still haunt the town? There are reports by local residents indicating that for such a small town, there does seem to be a lot of ghostly activity. One of the best known haunted locations in Athens is the Stewart House, which is just across the street from the river's edge. It was built as a hotel in 1883 by Hardy Stewart and he ran a very successful establishment.

The Stewart House

Stewart was so proud of his hotel that he had his name cast in iron at the main entrance. Unfortunately, the iron worker wasn't the best speller, as the letter "S" is backwards! (The current owner, Owen Lipstein, has decided to accentuate this quirk, and has incorporated the misdirected letter into all the logos on the restaurant, the tables, the menus, and it has even been set into the bricks by the garden pavilion.)

The backwards "S" at the hotel's doorstep.

Stewart House has a long history of famous and influential guests, which continues to this day. Now a restaurant and inn, Steven Spielberg dined here while making *War of the Worlds*, and one of the movie's stars, Dakota Fanning, stayed here during the filming of the ferry scene. Actress Meryl Streep "died" in one of the bedrooms during the filming of the movie *Iron Weed*. Many other notables come to dine at the fine restaurant, or stay in one of the rooms with the spectacular river views.

Hardy Stewart would probably be happy to know that his establishment is still in operation, and just perhaps, he knows from firsthand knowledge. It is difficult to say exactly what spirit is opening and closing the doors of the Stewart House in the dead of night, or who is making their voice echo down the corridors in the darkness, but Hardy is definitely a candidate, as one of the sound heard most often is that of someone walking up to a door fumbling for his keys.

Those employees who have experienced this assert that the keys do not make the sound of modern keys clinking together, which is actually a very astute observation. Instead, these keys sound like the clanking of a ring of old fashioned skeleton keys. As people often hear the footsteps and keys around closing time, some surmise that it's just Hardy still making sure his place is secure for the night.

Employees often hear someone walking past the bar room around closing time.

There's another strange thing involving keys in the Stewart House—they disappear. One staff member explained that she had just finished affixing new numbered tags to each of the keys for the nine guest rooms. They were hanging in order on a board, but a short time later, she noticed that the key to room #2 was missing. There was another woman working in the building that day, but that woman insisted she didn't take the key. She hadn't even been near the key board, and had no reason to take a room key.

The staff member searched high and low for two days, and finally gave up. She had to call a locksmith and when he arrived, she began to explain that a key had gone missing. As she spoke, she pointed to the key board, but as she did, she noticed that suddenly there was key #2 hanging in its proper place!

Naturally, someone could have been playing a prank, but this was not an isolated incident. Keys have disappeared when no one else was in the building, and have even gone missing from people's pockets. Some are found right away, but on average, the keys

The Stewart House is just across the street from the beautiful Hudson River.

reappear in odd places about two days later. Most recently, guests have begun to report that their room keys keep going missing, only to show up in the most unlikely places. Perhaps someone is playing a prank, just not someone they can actually see!

Other objects have also been witnessed moving on their own. One employee walked into a storage room and suddenly all the containers on just one shelf fell to the floor. It was as if someone had used their arm in a sweeping motion to push them off the shelf. Another night, several witnesses saw the corks pop out of a row of wine bottles. They replaced the corks, but as soon as they did, the corks came flying out of the bottles again. Had some natural pressure caused the corks to pop, once the pressure was relieved the corks should have stayed put.

The chef spends a lot of time at the restaurant, and has had his share of bizarre experiences. One day he stepped out into a hall and at the far end he saw a broom moving on its own. It was as if someone was sweeping the floor, but no one was visible! On a cold winter's day, he had just entered the Stewart House when a pipe burst over his head. He ran around the corner and another pipe burst above him. He had no idea where the shut off valve was in the basement, but when he ran downstairs he somehow managed to head straight for it. Had someone guided him to prevent further damage, or was it just luck?

The most recent event occurred just two weeks before writing this entry. A couple was spending the night, and the woman kept hearing someone pacing back and forth directly in front of her door. The man slept right through the night (what a surprise!), but the poor woman was so terrified she made sure the door was double locked and barely slept a wink.

Whatever spirit or spirits walk the halls of the Stewart House, they never appear to want to do any harm—mischief, perhaps, but no harm. If it is Hardy or some former employee, they seem to just want to go about their business and make sure the place is safe, secure, and clean.

If you need to escape from your busy life or are just looking for a unique experience, book yourself a stay at the Stewart House in the sleepy little town of Athens. Enjoy the beautiful river, dine in their award-winning restaurant, and spend the night in a movie star's room. If you do hear footsteps or doors closing in the night, just think of it as a paranormal security guard. Just keep an open mind, hang onto your keys, and think how envious your friends will be when you tell them you experienced firsthand what others only read about…

The dining room at the Stewart House has a tin ceiling and murals on the walls. Is Hardy Stewart still keeping watch here?

Ulster County Jail

The old Ulster County Jail on Golden Hill Road in Kingston.

On a weekend trip to Gettysburg in May, 2008, I didn't sleep well that Saturday night (due primarily to the noise from the high school prom taking place in the hotel, which the front desk conveniently neglected to tell us about when we made reservations). Needless to say, I was tired on Sunday and my husband, Bob, said I would just have to sleep late and take it easy on Monday.

"Oh no," I replied. "I have to get up early to go to jail."

"Which one?" came his matter-of-fact response, as if this was nothing out of the ordinary for me.

When you are a ghost investigator, such things aren't out of the ordinary. In fact, considering that just two weeks earlier I was in Eastern State Penitentiary again, such things are, well, commonplace. Prisons, murder and suicide sites, cemeteries, asylums—I get to go to all the best places, and I wouldn't trade it for anything!

This particular prison case came about thanks to a corrections officer, Hank VanDerBeck, who got in touch with me to share some of his experiences at the old Ulster County Jail on Golden Hill Road in Kingston, New York. In this instance, "old" is relative, as the jail was only opened in 1971. However, due to overcrowding and a poor original design, a new jail was built and occupied in 2007. That left the Golden Hill facility empty…or did it?

If we are to believe the eyewitness accounts of at least a dozen corrections officers over the span of about four years, then the old Ulster County Jail had more residents than appeared in their prisoner rosters, and there's no reason to believe that they left the building once the inmates were moved to the new facility. And how can we not trust what these specialized, professional men and women have seen?

As Hank so aptly put it, "I'm trained to carefully observe *everything* that's going on. I watch and listen for a living."

It's not exactly the fast track to career advancement for corrections officers to publicly go on record that they have seen things that can't be explained in any normal sense of reality. So it is quite remarkable that not only one such officer is willing to sign his name to the paranormal log book, but three other officers are willing to go on the record as well—Pat Meddors, Nicole Whitaker, and Ann Marie Legg. In addition, many other corrections officers and their supervisors also shared their bizarre experiences at the jail, but they prefer to remain anonymous, and as always, I will respect their privacy.

So, what exactly have these trained observers seen? A lot.

A lot of extraordinary apparitions and shadowy figures, almost exclusively between the hours of midnight at 4:30am. But while one might expect that such persistent and consistent activity would have been experienced for decades, it was only in the last four years that Hank began to have strange experiences.

"For the first twelve years I didn't notice anything unusual. I never even gave such things any thought," he said. "Then four years ago it all started happening, and at first I didn't tell anyone what I was seeing. But when others started to say what they witnessed, and it matched exactly what I had been seeing, I started to openly talk about it. I was fascinated and wanted to find out more about what was happening."

My first question upon hearing this was, "What had happened four years ago that might have provoked the start of this activity? Was there a significant incident or tragedy? Had major renovations taken place?"

There hadn't been any particular tragic incidents or renovations, but that didn't mean I was on the wrong track. Something of note had happened—the decision had been made to build a new jail and it had been announced that this building would eventually be vacated. This would not be the first case in my experience where the paranormal volume was jacked up in order to make an impression before living potential witnesses moved out.

As so many things have been seen by so many different people over the course of those four years, attempting a chronological report of activity would be difficult. Instead, I will present the accounts in three separate categories: the sightings of various male figures, the dark shadowy figures, and the mysterious and almost mystical woman in white. (Note: All of these reported sightings have been from staff working the night shifts.)

When approaching the old Ulster County Jail, it appears to be an ordinary government office building, unless you looked very closely at the vents over all of the windows and realized they were actually bars. Upon entering the front door, there are several typical offices. However, if you make your first left and walk down the hall, there's soon no question as to where you are. Industrial drab paint on concrete floors, doors and walls made of thick bars, bullet-proof glass, security cameras watching every inch—welcome to hell, county jail style.

I have to admit that at first I was under the impression that county jails were relatively low-key facilities where shoplifters and drivers caught under the influence spent the night. In reality, county jails are some of the toughest of prison facilities because *all* offenders are brought here, from the petty thief to the serial rapist, pedophiles, and murderers. This is where everyone is held until trial and sentencing, and then they are relocated to the proper state or federal prison. County jails are such intense, high stress places that the suicide rate is actually *nine times higher* than that of other types of jails. The bottom line is that these are bad places with very bad people.

The Ulster County Jail encompasses three tiers of cells, a one-story modular addition, rec rooms, sick bays, and maintenance rooms, all monitored from a central control area on the first floor. That control area leads directly into the female section of the jail, where a large percentage of the activity has occurred.

One night Pat Meddors was running her key card through a security check point in front of the door to the female section. Out of the corner of her eye she saw movement in the doorway, and as everyone was supposed to be in their cells, this was not a good thing. Turning to get a better look, she saw a man in his fifties, dressed in denim overalls and wearing a cap, peering around the edge of the door to see if anyone was coming. He looked mostly solid, and he clearly had distinct facial features and clothing.

"I took a few steps back, and just stared. All the hair went up on the back of my neck and arms," Pat explained as she pointed to the spot where the apparition had stood, not more than ten feet away. "Then he just disappeared and I tried to figure out what I had just seen."

Of course, she checked the entire female section and no one was out of their locked cell, and there certainly weren't any men. And being a jail, there were no other ways in or out, so no one could have been playing a joke.

On the second and third floors were the men's cells, and several different sightings of male figures occurred there. On the second floor, one of the corrections officers (who shall remain nameless) was making his rounds. The cells are in the center of the floor, and a hallway goes completely around all four sides, giving clear views down each long hall. The officer, who is known for being a by-the-book, no nonsense, stickler for details kind of guy, was turning the corner to walk down "D" corridor when he stopped dead in his tracks.

About half way down the corridor was the figure of man. The figure was only visible from the waist up (there were no legs) and he was floating near the ceiling in a grayish fog. The legless figure was moving slowly through the air toward the other end of the hall and it passed right through the ceiling, wall, and top of a heavy metal locked door to the emergency staircase. The officer admits he was

The doorway to the female section.

frozen in place as he watched this apparition moving, and understandably, he never reported the incident to his supervisor.

For some reason, there is a lot of activity connected with these doors on each of the three floors. Many figures and shadows have been witnessed moving both in and out of the cell blocks by passing through these locked doors. Is there some significance or naturally occurring energy in this area of the property that would account for the high number of sightings? Or is it simply that so many desperate prisoners focused their attention and energy on those doors, seeing them as their escape route to freedom?

One of the emergency doors where apparitions have been witnessed entering and exiting.

Unfortunately, there were several desperate prisoners who felt their only ticket to freedom was death. In fact, over the years about ten people committed suicide in their cells by hanging themselves with bed sheets. Another two or three prisoners died of natural causes. With at least a dozen deaths occurring within the walls of a place steeped in the negative energy of violence and depravity, it's no wonder that spirits still wander the halls and look for ways out.

The entrance to the A-B tier of cells on the second floor.

Another sighting of a male figure occurred at the doorway to the cell block on the other half of the second floor, and this time only legs were seen! One of the officers heard footsteps and saw something moving, so he turned and saw a man run past the doorway. By the time he looked, the man's torso (if he had one) had passed the doorway, but he clearly saw the legs and feet. Once again, after a thorough search, no explanation for the sighting was found.

On many occasions, footsteps are heard down the long halls, well after everyone has been locked into their individual cells at night. One of the incidents that stands out occurred when an officer was walking down the left side of the cell block and he heard footsteps coming from the right side. Hurrying across the back of the cell block he reached the right side, only to see nothing. Then the footsteps started on the left side. Hurrying down the front of the cell block he reached the left side, but once again saw nothing. Realizing this little game could go on all night, he just ignored the footsteps and they finally stopped.

While most of the sightings of male figures have been of those in ordinary clothing, Hank did see a man dressed in a "Class A" corrections officer's uniform, which has distinctive dark blue pants with a stripe down the side, as opposed to the standard khaki pants of the other officers. It was after 4:15am and he was expecting another officer to make a round of the cell block and swipe his security card. He waited, and waited, and wondered where the man could be.

Hank was sitting at a desk in the front right corner, so he had a clear view of anyone entering or exiting the doorway to the cell block, as well as an unobstructed line of sight down the right side corridor. He was quite surprised then, when through the bars at the back of the cell block he saw the striped pants of a uniform, and couldn't understand how he missed seeing the officer enter the cell block, and hadn't heard him walking, either.

The security device in which guards swipe their cards was at the far end of the right corridor, and while in the darkness Hank couldn't make out the officer's identity, he assumed it was the man he had been waiting for, and soon heard the familiar clicking sound the device makes when a card is swiped. Expecting the man to then proceed up the right corridor and say hello, he instead lost sight of the man. He waited a few seconds, then a few more, and finally went to see what the man was up to in the back of the cell block. Making a complete circuit of the cell block, he found no one.

One of the security card readers.

Hank then went to the adjoining cell block, found the officer he thought he had just seen and asked what was going on. Not understanding the question, the man apologized for being late. He got caught up in something else and hadn't yet had the time to come to Hank's cell block.

"What do you mean? You were just in there! I saw you and heard the card being swiped," Hank told the other officer.

The man continued to insist that he hadn't stepped foot in that cell block, and when Hank noticed that the officer was wearing khaki pants, he knew he was telling the truth. In fact, after going through the entire jail, he found that everyone on duty was wearing khaki pants. The most remarkable thing was that records indicated that *someone* had swiped the card at that security device at 4:27am, someone wearing dark striped pants who was not seen entering or exiting the cell block, and could not be found anywhere in the jail!

As fascinating as these sightings of male figures are, they literally pale in comparison to the dark shadows that move through the jail at night. Black shapes have been seen passing through walls and windows, and most often through those doors to the emergency stairwell.

For example, a supervisor was walking one of the corridors in the G and H section of cells (which housed the worst offenders) when he saw a completely dark figure emerge out of the wall from the emergency stairwell. It then turned and walked away from him and out of sight. He never found any explanation, and he also did not report the sighting and prefers to remain anonymous.

There had been a couple of suicides in the G section, and many officers have reported that this is the one area in the entire jail that made them feel very uneasy, even fearful. While walking their rounds, they would experience chills as they reached this corridor, and their hair would stand on end. This had nothing to do with any particular prisoners, because prisoners would come and go, but the frightening feeling always remained.

One night Hank was sitting behind a desk in the rec room, which had been converted into a sleeping quarters for about fifteen men. Some of the inmates told him about dark shadows that flew around the room and then went out the window. Naturally skeptical of anything a prisoner had to say, let alone something so bizarre, Hank simply replied, "Yeah, sure."

However, seeing is definitely believing, as Hank was to discover that night. Everyone was asleep, the place was quiet, and it looked as though it would be an uneventful shift. Then to his right, coming out of the wall, were two large, dark shapes. He described them as being about three to four feet wide and tapered on the ends "like footballs." They moved swiftly through the air, and it was like one was chasing the other. After a few seconds they both shot right out through one of the barred windows.

He knew he was not dreaming, but could there be some rational explanation? He checked outside to see if anything could have been moving by the parking lot lights to create the strange effect, and he checked the hallway, the wall, and the window. There was simply no way to explain what he had just witnessed, and what he now knew to be the truth of what many inmates had been seeing.

Another night Hank was at his desk and he kept trying to brush something off the back of his shoulders. He couldn't quite describe the sensation, but he kept feeling that something was touching him. There was just a wall behind him, and he never saw anything when he turned around. The next morning a couple of inmates started talking to him about the "things" that had been behind him that night. They went on to describe seeing two dark shadows floating above him, and every once in a while one would appear to reach down and touch Hank's back!

Not that paranormal activity is ever straightforward, but activity is particularly puzzling here with so many things being seen floating and moving through the air near the ceilings. Also, there are so many sightings, particularly of the dark shapes that move through walls, doors, and windows with seemingly no regard to the layout of the structure.

It's not that the movements of any apparitions ever appear to be in any way hampered by the physical world, but in a lot of cases where the activity is linked to a former resident, spirits are seen moving down the halls, staircases, and through the open doorways of the home they remember. In other words, whatever is flying through the air and walls of the jail doesn't seem to have any memory of the place. Does this indicate that whatever is here, was here on this land long before the jail was built?

In the case of the mysterious woman in white, I personally do feel this is the case, but please form your own opinion after reading the following accounts:

A female officer passed by a long room with two doors about twenty feet apart. The room contained female prisoners who started calling for the nurse when she passed by again a few minutes later. Thinking something was wrong, she asked who needed a nurse. They said they wanted their medications from the nurse who had just been walking with her.

"What are you talking about? The nurse was here an hour ago, and I was walking by myself," the female officer insisted.

However, the prisoners were just as insistent. Through the windows of both doors, they had seen a woman in a white dress walking directly behind the officer, and assumed it was the nurse. It wasn't, but what or who it was is just possibly the greatest mystery of the activity here.

Hank was in the modular addition, once again sitting at a desk keeping an eye on all the prisoners as they slept. Suddenly, there was a misty light to his right, between him and the wall that was just a few away. Shifting his eyes to the right, he saw a woman's hand and an outstretched arm draped in a white robe or gown of a silky, flowing material. He could see the side of her body as well, from the torso to the floor, also covered by the robe. He described the hand as one with long fingers and flawless, milky white skin. It appeared to be a solid human hand, but the garment was something entirely unnatural.

"The fabric glowed with a brilliant light of its own. It was as bright as a 200 watt bulb. I turned to try to see her face, but she vanished."

How did Hank react to this particular apparition?

"I felt a kind of euphoria. And the best way I can describe her appearance is like one of those statues of the Virgin Mary with her arms outstretched."

A saint-like figure in a county jail? Clearly this doesn't fit with any known circumstances or people connected with the jail, and most likely is not connected to the structure. And while no one is claiming this is a miraculous apparition, it may be connected to another Mary.

Supposedly, sometime early in the twentieth century, a girl or young woman drowned in a pond in Kingston. That pond became known as Mary's Pond, which is literally a stone's throw from the walls of the jail. At least as early as the 1930s, local residents claimed to see a "Lady in White" or a "Lady of the Lake" by Mary's Pond. Did the jail simply "inherit" this lady when it was built on "her" property?

There is another possibility to consider, as well. Is it indeed the figure of the poor drowned girl that is seen in the jail, or did the story of the drowning arise to try to explain the sightings? In some cases, the apparitions pre-date the alleged tragedies, and it must be considered that this beautiful, glowing, mystical woman may have some connection to this property that goes back much farther than anyone can remember.

There have been many other sightings of the Lady in White. In fact, she is the figure seen most frequently by the most witnesses.

While typically the Lady in White is just glimpsed moving past the doorway to the female section, one night Ann Marie saw a woman in a gown just standing in the open doorway, looking her way. The figure was complete, although she didn't notice the facial features. The figured remained for a few seconds, then turned and walked away. Once again, what was most noticeable (or perhaps enchanting is more the word?) were the flowing folds of the glowing gown. Ann Marie was to see the Lady in White on two other occasions, as well.

There is also inexplicable activity that does not fall directly into the three main categories described above. For example, one night Pat was on constant watch of two suicidal women. One had slit her wrists earlier in the day, the other had claimed that she would kill herself. Sitting in front of the women's cells throughout the long night, she took a moment to rest her head in her hand. Suddenly she felt a finger in the middle of her forehead that literally pushed her head upright.

Thinking someone had caught her as her attention had begun to wander, she turned around and fully expected to see her supervisor. No one was there. She did a quick check of the entire floor and found no one, and she realized she hadn't heard the sound of the heavy entrance door open or close, so nobody had left.

Had she just been in that twilight state between waking and sleeping and imagined that her head was being pushed? It was possible, so she was determined to not put her head in her hands again and made sure she was sitting up straight and wide awake. However, the time crept slowly by, and she just wanted to close her eyes for a moment. The second she did, a male voice spoke directly into her ear.

"Hey!"

This time Pat was sure her supervisor was standing right behind her. She was also sure she was fully awake when she heard the voice, but once again, she found that she was alone. Was one of the spirits just having some fun with her, or were they helping her to stay awake to prevent yet another suicide?

Other officers have also reported hearing voices and sounds for which they couldn't find any source. These sounds, as well as the sightings of the figures and shadows, greatly increased in frequency in the months before the jail was closed. Again, it was as if the spirits knew they didn't have much more time to make their presence known. But what was the point of all this activity; was there some particular message they were trying to get across? Do they need help being released from this place? We would see if we could get any answers during our investigation on a Friday the 13th in the summer of 2008.

The view down a long cell block to the emergency door.

My first visit to the jail was during the day several weeks

earlier, and it was simply to have a look around and get some pictures. Even though it was a sunny morning, there was a dark atmosphere to the cell blocks, and I knew being there at night would just serve to amplify all those feelings. I was actually surprised when we obtained permission to conduct a full investigation at night, but I guess that my track record and the fact that Mike is a cop helped to demonstrate that we were responsible people who took this work seriously.

A typical cell.

There was great anticipation in the days before the investigation. This was an amazing opportunity to try to collect evidence in a place where many trained observers had repeatedly witnessed the same phenomena. Would we see or photograph any anomalies, would we hear any sounds, would we come face to face with the Lady in White? These were exciting possibilities, and clearly Mike and I needed to fortify ourselves for the long night ahead of us, so I made a big batch of brownies for the trip up to the jail. (Ghost Investigators do not live by meters and cameras alone, you know.)

Our group that night would consist of Hank and his wife, Pat and her girlfriend, and a county law enforcement officer and his daughter. We set up "base camp" in the former visitation room near the central area. The plan was simple—start with the female section on the first floor, then work our way up and just see what happened, and then adjust accordingly, if necessary.

Mike and I set up camcorders in the female cell block, while the group sat in the hall just outside the doorway. Things were fairly quiet in the cell block, but I was called back to the hall as they were hearing things out there. I grabbed my camera and digital recorder and headed back to the central area. Just before stepping through the doorway, there was a loud banging noise in the ceiling above me. The digital recorder captured the following:

Bang, bang.
"All right, knocking sounds right above me."
Bang.
"Again."
BANG!

I sound remarkably calm at that moment, even though I'm standing in a haunted jail and something is making an unholy racket just over my head. In fact, I was far more curious than scared, but that changed in a heartbeat. What didn't get recorded for some reason, but what I clearly heard a few moments later, was a host of whispering voices in front of me. It was like a crowd of people, male and female, all speaking low, about fifteen feet ahead.

Still, my fascination level was high, until the voices started moving toward me, and I heard the shuffle of dozens of feet. Instinctively I started stepping backward as the sounds came closer. It was an intensely creepy and overwhelming feeling, and I became very concerned about what would happen when these sounds caught up to me and engulfed me.

Fortunately, that didn't happen, because as I backed through the doorway the voices and shuffling feet suddenly stopped. I waited breathlessly for a moment or two, then gingerly stepped back through the door. Nothing. Whatever this group had been trying to impress upon me, I guess they had decided they had made their point. And believe me, I was duly impressed!

Pat then came up the hall to see if I was okay. The group (of the living) had seen me backing up and wondered what had happened. I told everyone what had just occurred, and lest they think I was completely crazy, played back the banging noises I had recorded. Those sounds were most likely just the bait to get me alone in the central area and then demonstrate just what we were dealing with here—a lot of wandering souls, and a hell of a night ahead of us!

Now before anyone thinks that what I was hearing was just the air conditioning making strange noises, I must point out that there wasn't any air conditioning, or fans, or anything else. Also, before setting up equipment in a cell block, we first cut the power to it so there wouldn't be any question that any sounds we heard or EMF readings we got were not natural.

On the second floor, we set up camcorders both inside the row of cells and in the hallway. There were two cell blocks per floor on the second and third floors, mirror images on either side of a central hall. In other words, there was a lot of ground to cover. On the first floor, Mike and Pat had been trying to provoke some paranormal action (in fact, Mike was trying to stir things up in the female section as I was experiencing the sounds in the central area), and that provocation continued for a while. However, it was when things got quiet that things really began to happen.

I set up my digital recorder at the far end of a cell block hall by the emergency staircase door. Mike chose to sit right in front of a cell in the middle of the block, and Hank and his wife sat by a cell at a table in the front of the block. The rest of us stayed in the hallway at the very front of the tier. In other words, Mike was about 30 feet from the nearest person, and my recorder was probably about 50 feet beyond him.

Everything was relatively quiet, just a few knocking sounds here or there, when suddenly Mike got up and hurried down the cell

The tables in the enclosed area in front of the cells.

block. He didn't even stop when he reached the hall, he continued right out of the tier, saying he had to get out of there. I knew that meant something serious had happened, so I hurried after him. He was sitting in the central hall, looking as though he had just been through a terrible ordeal.

"Are you okay? Do you want to tell me what happened?" I asked, then waited while he took a few deep breaths.

"I had trouble breathing…it felt like I was being strangled…then this awful feeling came over me…I had to get out of there because it felt like I wasn't going to be able to take another breath," Mike said, as the look in his eyes told me this was no joke.

I told him to just take it easy, and not to come back in that tier. He didn't argue.

The county law enforcement officer and his daughter who had been with us earlier had left before this incident. Later, when Hank was telling this man about Mike's experience in front of that particular cell, the cell number rang a bell—a prisoner had committed suicide by hanging himself right where Mike had been sitting, feeling as though he was being strangled to death! This demonstrates that while it pays to be sensitive in the ghost hunting field, sometimes you have to pay a very high price for that sensitivity.

The surprises didn't end there, however, as a few days later when reviewing the audio files I discovered something equally shocking that had been recorded on the digital recorder by the locked emergency exit. I could clearly hear the distant echo of our voices from the other end of the tier. Then suddenly, very close to the microphone, was the distinct sound of sighing or exhaling, twice. The sounds came as a startling contrast to the rest of the recording. I focused my attention even more on the audio file, and a few moments later there was something that *really* made my blood run cold.

"Sa…rah…"

I practically jumped out of my seat when I heard the name whispered, and it sounded as if the person was right next to the recorder. I played that section of audio over and over again to make sure I wasn't imagining it, but there it was in all its chilling clarity; a man's voice whispering the name Sarah.

I immediately copied the recording to my computer and sent the clip to Hank and Mike. I needed their opinion of the mysterious voice. Both of them got right back to me, agreeing that they also heard the name Sarah. Shortly after, I spoke to Hank on the phone, and he asked why I thought a woman's name had been whispered in this male section of the jail. I speculated that perhaps one of the men who had committed suicide here had a wife or girlfriend named Sarah, and that he had spoken her name with his last breath. Little did I realize how close to the truth I actually was with this theory.

The three audio clips (the banging, sighing, and Sarah) were soon circulating among the jail staff, but no one had an explanation for the woman's name being spoken. Then about a month later, Hank was discussing the subject with two other corrections officers. One of the men was an "old-timer," having worked at the jail for over twenty years, several years longer than Hank. After hearing the story of the audio, he said, "There's only one Sarah I know that has any connection to that jail." The story he went on to tell was startling.

One day, twenty years ago, this guard had watched over a prisoner who had been granted a request to phone his wife. The purpose of the call was forgiveness, with the prisoner being the one begging for forgiveness for the awful things he had done. His crimes had been among the most despicable a man could commit—for years he had been molesting his own daughter.

The guard overheard the prisoner repeatedly asking his wife to tell the daughter how sorry he was, and he begged for forgiveness from both of them, over and over again. The name of the daughter, and the name that the prisoner kept saying throughout the conversation, was Sarah.

When the prisoner hung up the phone, the guard noticed that he had an odd smile; a peaceful, almost contented look had come over him. The guard led the man back to his cell, and that would be the last time he saw him alive. Within an hour after the call of forgiveness for his crimes against his daughter, the man committed suicide by hanging himself, and the name of Sarah was no doubt the last word to pass his lips…

When Hank relayed this story to me I felt a chill from head to foot. Here was the smoking gun, the link to tie together a tragic episode in the jail from twenty years ago, and a bizarre voice whispered and recorded in the dead of night. Is this man still seeking forgiveness even in death? Did he want us to know how sorry he was for the horrible things he did? The pieces of this awful puzzle do all seem to fit together. But I'm not about to pat myself on the back for this one. As remarkable as it is, the nature of the crimes and events still leaves me feeling sick about it all.

Of course, at the time of the investigation, all we knew was that Mike had a rough time of it, but was willing to continue. The strange sounds also continued in the darkness around us, and on many occasions we had the strong feeling that we were not alone. At no point was that experience so strong as when we were all in the third floor rec room, turned dormitory, where Hank had seen the black shadows flying through the air.

It was close to 2am, and we were all sitting at a table taking a short break. Suddenly, there were other voices echoing up the central staircase, and the sounds of people moving around. It seemed as if these people were on the first floor. I asked Hank who else had a key, and he couldn't think of anyone else who would have access,

The table where we all sat in the rec room on the third floor.

or why they would be showing up at an empty jail in the middle of the night. Pat looked out the window, but couldn't see any other cars in the parking lot. We listened for a few more moments, and all agreed that the voices and sounds of movement were unmistakable.

"If they are ghosts, this is one of the most remarkable things I've ever heard," I said, then thought again. "And if they aren't ghosts, all of our equipment is down there!"

I suppose I should have let the two corrections officers or the cop go first, but my curiosity and my concern for our equipment made me jump to my feet and rush to the stairwell. I shouted down the stairs to see if I could get a response, and when no one answered I just took off running. I don't know if I even gave a thought as to what I might be running into—some potentially dangerous intruders, or some of the noisiest ghosts on record.

I continued to call out for someone to respond as I passed the second floor, then descended to the first floor. I ran straight into the base camp room, and spun around to do a quick check to make sure all the equipment cases were still there. A second or two later I was off and running again, this time heading for the front door. No one was in sight, either inside or out, and I didn't see any car lights driving away. The front door had been locked, but when I gave it a shove, it swung wide open!

Still dealing with the possibility that this was not paranormal, that we were dealing with some kind of intruders, I started doubling back. The group joined me and we made a room by room search of the jail from top to bottom, but found no one. We simply couldn't understand what had happened. We all heard the voices loud and clear, but there was no sign of anyone, and the locked door was now open. And I'm certain that if there's one thing a prison guard knows how to do, it is lock a door!

After the search, we made sure the door was once again locked and went back up to the third floor dorm room. We were all quite stunned, and tried to come up with some rational explanations. We did arrive at a conclusion, but not as the result of any discussion, at least not from any of us.

A couple of minutes after we had gathered back in that room, we clearly heard the voices and sounds coming up the staircase again! It was as if several men were talking and going about their business, whatever business that may have been. I was completely fascinated by this persistent, in-your-face paranormal activity, and could have stayed there listening all night. However, when the voices started again, Mike declared, "That's it, I'm out of here."

I was surprised, but I hadn't realized how shaken he had been by the choking episode. No investigation is worth being traumatized –I've been there, done that, too many times—so despite all the activity, we made the wise decision to pack up and go. As soon as we started heading downstairs, the voices and movement stopped, but I have no doubt they all picked up again where they left off as soon as we left the building.

It was good to get outside and into the fresh air, and for the first time I realized how worn out I was, too. It had been several hours of almost relentless experiences, culminating in a mad dash into the midst of who knows what. By the time I got home and to sleep it was almost morning, but just two short hours later I was up and active—obviously the result of far too much adrenaline being pumped into my system that night.

In the days and weeks that followed, we went over all the audio and video. Aside from the three clips I've already discussed, there were many other banging and knocking sounds. I started out by writing the time each sound occurred on the tape, and finally gave up as there had been just too many. All in all, the old Ulster County Jail has to rank among the top haunted places I have ever been!

The one disappointment, however, was that I didn't see the Lady in White. I don't know why I am so intrigued by this entity, but she does sound like something far beyond the usual run-of-the-mill spirit. There is a great mystery and enchantment about her, and I someday hope to discover her secret.

I did obtain one more fascinating piece of the puzzle several weeks later. My suspicions that she was not connected with the jail were confirmed when Hank called to share some new information. He was attending a graduation party of a neighbor's daughter, when the subject of ghosts came up. Before he could tell his story, a neighbor mentioned some strange experiences where she worked, which just happened to be at the clinic which is on the property next to the old Ulster County Jail.

She said that she and many other people had witnessed a woman in white walking the halls of the clinic. The most remarkable thing about this woman was that the fabric of her garment glowed with a light of its own!

So there it was, the enigmatic Lady in White has also been seen in the building next to the jail, and therefore is most likely tied to this entire area through some unknown event from long before these places were built. Where else has she been seen? For how many generations has she been walking this land, with her glowing robe captivating the living? I must know more about this almost saint-like figure, and I will continue on with this aspect of the investigation.

I would also like to get back into the jail some night. Mike and I have already discussed a strategy for making sure we would be alerted to any intruders, and we would also keep cameras running on the first floor to capture any spiritual visitors, as well. One thing neither of us will be doing, however, is sitting on any suicide sites—we've both had our fill of those experiences!

Who knows what other information may someday come to light about this place and the surrounding land? And who knows what will ultimately happen to the old jail? County officials are currently discussing possible uses for the structure, so most likely it won't be demolished.

All I know is that a frightening haunted jail is a terrible thing to waste…

Author's Note: About two months after the investigations, I was thinking about that voice saying "Sarah," when something hit me. In 2003, I wrote a novel called *Dead Center*. The story is about a ghost hunter, named Sarah Brooks, who is called in to investigate a haunted shopping mall that may have been built over a Civil War battlefield. In one scene, Sarah is alone in the basement of this mall when she hears her name being whispered from a voice coming up out of the floor, just like on the recording. I can't imagine how there could be any connection, but the coincidence is so freaky I had to mention it. I had better be careful what I write in the future.

Sins of the Father

There are biblical references about the sins of the father affecting his children. Today, such a concept is generally only viewed in terms of financial or legal matters—for example, large debts incurred or shady deals that were made that would taint the image of future generations. But what if there was some truth to it? What if an angry and vengeful spirit tracked down the descendants of his enemy to torment them?

In January of 2008, psychic Lisa Ann received an email from a woman, let's call her Tina, requesting help with a haunting. As Lisa Ann doesn't want to have any prior knowledge of a location and its activity, she asked if I would call Tina to see if there was a credible case, and if so, gauge how critical was the situation. I spoke to Tina that same morning, and found her story both credible and urgent.

Tina is of Irish descent with a strong sixth sense flowing through the female line. From the age of three, she has encountered spirits that have often been very frightening. She knew she was seeing things that others couldn't, but rather than encourage her abilities, her strict Catholic parents told her there were no such things as ghosts. Instead of recognizing their daughter's talent and helping her to cope with it, they told her she had mental problems and to just ignore what she was seeing. Unfortunately, this attitude created a conflict between her religious beliefs and her spiritual inclinations, which could and should have complement one another.

Suffice to say, the years to come proved challenging. Fortunately, she married a good man, also Irish, but even with that union the turmoil created between the two sides of the family cast a shadow over their lives. However, whatever shadows were produced by the petty squabbles of the living were nothing in comparison to what the dead had in store for them.

While living in a townhouse in New York's Hudson Valley, they encountered a wide array of terrifying paranormal activity. The culminating event came one evening when Tina was upstairs saying her prayers with their two young children, and her husband was downstairs in the living room.

A faint, strange sound could be heard upstairs and then throughout the house, and it rapidly grew in intensity until it was like the deafening roar of an enormous wild animal. Her son started screaming, thinking there was a lion in the house. Tina was terrified, and while her first thought was to get her kids to safety, she found she was unable to move. Downstairs, her husband also felt as if his limbs were frozen and he couldn't get up from the couch, even though every instinct told him he had to save his family.

Tina prayed to her deceased father for help, and just as suddenly as the paralyzing effect had hit, it abated. Springing to her feet, she grabbed her children to get them away from the source of the horrible noise. Looking back years later, she is still absolutely certain that "someone" helped carry the children, but as her husband was downstairs, it couldn't have been him. She has no idea if the helping hands were those of her father, but it is most likely that in her most desperate moment of need some force of good stepped in to protect her family.

When her husband was finally able to move, he pulled the security alarm to summon the police, but this was clearly an event outside of their jurisdiction. As they were all about to run out of the house, Tina turned back to look up the stairs and saw something she will never forget.

"It looked like the devil," she said with an expression that spoke to the fear that still haunts her to this day. "It's the only way I can describe it, it looked like the devil."

Of course, the police found nothing. Shortly after, a psychic performed a cleansing on the townhouse and claimed that the spirit of a woman who resided there agreed to leave. However, the spirit of an agreeable woman does not fit the "profile" of an evil male entity hell bent on terrorizing the entire family. It was a happy day in 1998 when the family moved out of that townhouse.

They bought a house in a quiet town near Poughkeepsie, N.Y., and it came to be theirs in an unusual way. A man had put a down payment on the place, but just one week before closing he died in a car accident. Not the most auspicious beginning, but at least they now had a beautiful home with a yard for the kids. Everything was happy, calm, and peaceful the first six months, but all of that changed in a heartbeat.

One night the door from the garage suddenly swung open and triggered the security alarm. Tina's husband grabbed his gun and went to confront the intruder. No one was there, and when the police arrived they didn't find any footprints in the snow, so no person could have broken into the house.

After the police left, Tina turned to her husband and said, "He's back." She could just feel that whatever had tormented them at their townhouse had found them in their new home. Unfortunately, she was right, and the haunted activity began all over again.

Heavy footsteps would go up and down the staircase, voices could be heard, objects were thrown, and her daughter was choked to the point that red marks were visible on her throat. The television and other electronic equipment turned on and off by itself, and there were bitterly cold spots throughout the house. And for all of you who have repeatedly heard that ghosts can't harm you, consider this potentially fatal episode:

One day when Tina was eight months pregnant with their third child, she was standing in the upstairs hallway. Out of the blue—or perhaps out of the darkness would be more accurate—someone shoved her hard from behind. Reeling forward, she hit the banister, which broke loose. Just a spilt second before she would have fallen two stories, her husband lunged forward and managed to grab her with one hand, just tightly enough to pull her back. Had he not been there at that moment, it would have been an awful tragedy.

This is how Tina and her family have been living the last ten years. And with each passing year the toll on her family becomes more evident. Out of the house, they are all happy and have a good time together, but within the walls of their home some dark force inexorably affects everyone's personality. It's no way to live when the dead are intent on doing harm.

It was a cold morning in January when Mike, Lisa Ann, and I headed for Tina's house. As usual, the topic of conversation was on everything but the investigation that lay ahead. I hadn't told Lisa Ann anything about Tina's story, but as soon as we pulled into the driveway Lisa Ann felt a wave of nausea—not a good sign, but not surprising given what I already knew.

The house itself is a very nice upscale home that is tastefully decorated, but of course, appearances can be deceiving. Upon entering the house, Lisa Ann looked to her right into the living room, and in a mirror hanging on the far wall she saw a dark figure of a man passing back and forth behind her.

"There's a strong male presence," she said without a moment's hesitation. "This one I do get a threatening feeling from, an intimidating spirit. This one is not a happy little spirit, it's intimidating."

I knew she was comparing this experience to the benign spirits she experienced just a few days earlier at the Borland House. Again, I didn't expect this one would be pleasant, and the palpable hostility suggested it would only get worse. If there's one thing I've learned, nasty spirits don't appreciate having their dirty little secrets revealed.

We continued walking through the rooms on the first floor, and it was interesting to see how Lisa Ann's body language spoke volumes about what she was experiencing. Unlike the relaxed nature of the Borland House investigation, she was now tense and on guard, and for good reason.

"He's angry, because somebody took something from him, either his land or his money."

However, as strong as the impressions were, she couldn't see the connection between this man and the house. As we ascended the stairs to the second floor, Lisa Ann began gritting her teeth and spoke about the anger level rising with each step.

"I don't like kids," she said, verbally forwarding the messages she was receiving from the angry man. "And I really don't like people, either, to be honest with you."

Describing the man as "thickly built" and having some connection to construction, she began to pace back and forth as she felt this spirit often does, and repeated that somebody took something from him and owes him a lot of money. And clearly there was something perplexing about this man.

Lisa Ann describes the angry man to me.
(Photo by Michael Worden.)

"I came from somewhere else," Lisa Ann said, her features mirroring both the agitated state of the man and the confusing nature of his role in this haunting.

"You mean from another country?" I asked.

"No. In other words, I'm not really connected to this house or the property, but I came here, like spirit-wise, I came here. Maybe that means he followed the people who live here?"

I resisted the impulse to shout, "Bingo!"

"I just don't think he was ever in this house [when he was living], and I don't feel he's connected to this land. The land I see him connected with is a large piece of land. And I keep hearing the Hatfields and the McCoys."

[Author's Note: The famous feud between these two families in Kentucky and West Virginia has become a classic symbol for enraged conflicts between two factions, especially families.]

"I almost feel that this is connected to one of them and their families that goes way back. Like somebody screwed somebody and now that spirit follows the other family. It is not a connection with the house or land, it is a connection with the people who live here," she finally was able to state definitively as the message became clearer. "This place isn't like any other we've been to because of that tie with the people, not the location."

We next went into the master bedroom and it was like crossing the threshold into another world. Instead of anger and agitation, there was a peaceful serenity.

"I don't think he can come in here," Lisa Ann said as she visibly relaxed. "There's a totally different energy in here."

It wasn't clear why "he" couldn't enter, but there were quite a few religious items in the room, although later Lisa Ann said that while they were an annoyance to the entity—who realized they were placed around the house to keep him away—they probably weren't a complete deterrent.

When we stepped back into the hallway, I almost gasped at the shocking difference to the feel of the place. I asked if it could have anything to do with the way the staircase angled up to the second floor, kind of a large, squared-off spiral staircase, if that makes sense. I have dealt with a many haunted locations where activity appears to be concentrated around staircases, particularly spiral ones.

Lisa Ann felt that was part of it, along with the position of the windows, lights, mirrors, vents, etc., that bounced the energy around the open center hall. We went into a few of the other rooms, but Lisa Ann continued to be drawn to the top of the staircase, and she continued to speak as the angry male spirit.

"This reminds me of another staircase. When I look at it, and don't see it as it is, I see it as it was in that other place."

She/He went on to describe an old bar or brothel that he visited, a place "like something out of an old western movie." As he exited one of the upstairs rooms in this place, another man coming up the stairs confronted him, possibly because of jealousy, and a fight ensued. (At the moment she said the word "fight," the EMF meter went up.) The scene was confusing for a few moments, and it was difficult to see who pushed who, but slowly the episode from the past became clear.

There were high EMF readings by the banister where Tina had been pushed.

Lisa Ann was able to say that the angry male spirit had been the one in life who had pushed his enemy down the stairs, and was subsequently arrested and put in jail. As a result, the angry man lost his land, and forever blamed the man he pushed for what he saw as an injustice. Perhaps it had been an act of self-defense, perhaps others had conspired against him, or perhaps, he was at fault. Whatever the actual circumstances, the events ignited a thirst for vengeance that still has not been quenched.

It was all something Lisa Ann had never experienced before, and hadn't even known was possible—because this entity was so strong and had held onto this anger and bitterness for so long, he was somehow able to transfer the energy and memory of the fight to this house. The emotions of that distant action were now impressed onto this place. The episode of Tina being pushed through the banister began to make more sense.

I asked for more clarification as to the time and location of the original events, and Lisa Ann felt it was about three generations earlier, which meant the man who had been pushed down the stairs had most likely been either Tina's or her husband's great-grandfather.

As for the location, "I keep going south, and then going west, south, and then west," she replied, somewhat irritated that she couldn't place it more accurately. "But I don't see any cowboy hats so I don't think it was way out west. It was a small town, and this man had a lot, so people were jealous and just waiting for a reason to run him out of town. I don't know if these people [Tina and her family] have ever had trouble somewhere else that they lived, but he would follow them."

It was with mixed feelings that I listened to this information. For purely intellectual reasons I was fascinated and thrilled by the affirmations—yes, the family had sensed an angry male spirit they felt was following them. On the other hand, I was not insensitive to what this meant—an entity who could not let go of his rage was tormenting innocent people, just because they were descended from a man he believed had wronged him. This was an extraordinary case, but even as the pieces of the puzzle fell into place the big questions still remained—how could the family free themselves of his wrath?

When it came time for Lisa Ann to summarize her findings to Tina, we all gathered in the kitchen. As Lisa Ann spoke, you could see that Tina was practically busting at the seams wanting to confirm everything she was saying, but she waited until the summary was complete.

"Can I talk now?" she asked, then gave a deep sigh of relief as it was finally her turn to divulge the details of everything that had been happening to her and her family.

One of the first pieces of information she revealed—and one I hadn't heard before—was that she felt the angry spirit was connected to her side of the family, as a result of a dark family secret. Her grandfather had been a founding member of the Irish Republican Army, and a lot of blood was on his hands. As he was dying, he had apologized to Tina for all the suffering and death he had caused, and his actions certainly hung like a great weight on her conscience.

While such a violent past could haunt family members, it didn't fit the scenario that Lisa Ann had so clearly seen—a man in the southern or western United States, three generations ago, who had lost property due to a fight in a brothel. Could this possibly be reconciled with a member of the IRA in Ireland two generations ago? Unless this was all the result of some deeper pattern repeating itself across generations, it did appear as though these were two separate and distinct sets of circumstances. Perhaps there were more levels of retribution than could be seen?

As Tina spoke of her guilt about her grandfather, Lisa Ann felt that it was the energy of this guilt—along with the potent energy of fear—that helped feed the vengeful entity and made him strong. Of course, simply telling someone not to be afraid or guilty is much easier said than done. Also, learning how to shut down one's psychic abilities to protect against negative spirits is not so simple, especially under these unique circumstances.

Realizing a solution would take a multi-angled approach, Lisa Ann suggested some concrete actions to take, such as performing a cleansing of the house inside and out with sage and sea salt, and covering or removing the mirrors and light sources in the central hall. Tina said that they had a priest come in to do a blessing, but he refused to go upstairs. Tina and her friend then performed their own cleansing, but it only seemed to aggravate the spirit. Lisa Ann then provided the analogy of an alcoholic relative who is furious the first time that no drinks are served, and eventually just stops coming to the house.

This is a very important point to understand for people trying to rid their houses of unwanted guests, of the dead variety. Don't feed them the energy they need, keep performing cleansings that remove their sources of support, and stick with it. Remember, *you have the power to control these situations*. A haunting is all about the people who live there. It's your home, fight for it and take it back!

Lisa Ann had several other suggestions, so I decided to write down a "Plan of Action." An investigation can be a stressful experience for a homeowner, and with so much information coming out, it's difficult to remember everything that's said, so writing down findings and recommendations can help people cope once you've gone.

An interesting thing occurred as we all discussed the details of how to cleanse the house, and the importance of being persistent and taking back your own power. There was a low rumbling sound coming up from the basement. The sound grew louder and the floor beneath our feet actually began to shake. Mike started getting very high EMF readings. It was like an earthquake rattling the whole house, and then it all abruptly stopped. This was clearly one pissed off entity who did not like the idea of doing anything to drive him away, which made it all the more imperative that the Plan of Action be undertaken ASAP.

By the time we left, Tina seemed determined to gather her strengths to once and for all break this angry spirit's hold on her and her family. We can only hope she has persevered, for her sake, and for the sake of future generations.

It is truly a frightening thought to contemplate the possibility that something from the past—and not even your own past—can hunt you down wherever you go. Just remember, though, that you have the ability to loosen the grip of such spirits. You may need help, and it may take a while, but you owe it to yourself and the people you love to hang tough and drive negative energies out of your home.

Let's just hope that the sins of the father never come back to haunt you…

To order books, get info, and share your haunting, contact the Ghost Investigator through:

www.ghostinvestigator.com

Or write to:

Linda Zimmermann
P.O. Box 192
Blooming Grove, NY 10914

Or send email to:

linda@gotozim.com

Copy this page to use for your own ghost hunt. If you know of a haunted site you think should be considered for an upcoming book, please contact me at:

P.O. Box 192, Blooming Grove, NY, 10914

www.ghostinvestigator.com

Field Report

Date: **Location:**

Time In: **Weather:**

Names of People Interviewed:

Equipment: Camera ☐   Video ☐   Audio Recorder ☐   Thermometer   Other:

Experiences: Sounds ☐   Odors ☐   Cold Spots ☐   Visuals ☐   Touch/Sensations ☐   Movement ☐

Details (Attach extra sheet if necessary):

Time Out: **Total Time on Site:**

Conclusions:

Prepared and Signed by:

Witness(es):

Happy (Ghost) Hunting!

Other books by Linda Zimmermann

Dead Center
A Ghost Hunter Novel

When one of the country's largest shopping centers is built in Virginia, rumors abound that the place is haunted by ghosts of Civil War soldiers. Ghost hunter Sarah Brooks must uncover the truth, and come face to face with the restless spirits that walk through the *Dead Center*.

Okay, Sarah Brooks. This is what you do, she said to herself. *This is who you are.*

Closing her eyes, Sarah spun around and counted to three. When she opened her eyes, she had to clamp her hand over her mouth to stifle a scream. There was a pale, misty shape of a man drawing closer. It was like an image being projected into a fog, and it rippled, wavered, then slowly began to take on a more defined shape. The wounded man behind her screamed as if Death himself was coming to take him…

Ghost Investigator Volume 1: *Hauntings of the Hudson Valley*
Ghost Investigator Volume 2: *From Gettysburg to Lizzie Borden*
Ghost Investigator Volume 3
Ghost Investigator Volume 4: *Ghosts of New York and New Jersey*
Ghost Investigator Volume 5: *From Beyond the Grave*
Ghost Investigator Volume 6: *Dark Shadows*
Ghost Investigator Volume 7: *Psychic Impressions*

www.ingramcontent.com/pod-product-compliance
Ingram Content Group UK Ltd.
Pitfield, Milton Keynes, MK11 3LW, UK
UKHW041427180426
11947UKWH00007B/325